Maths 6 Ches

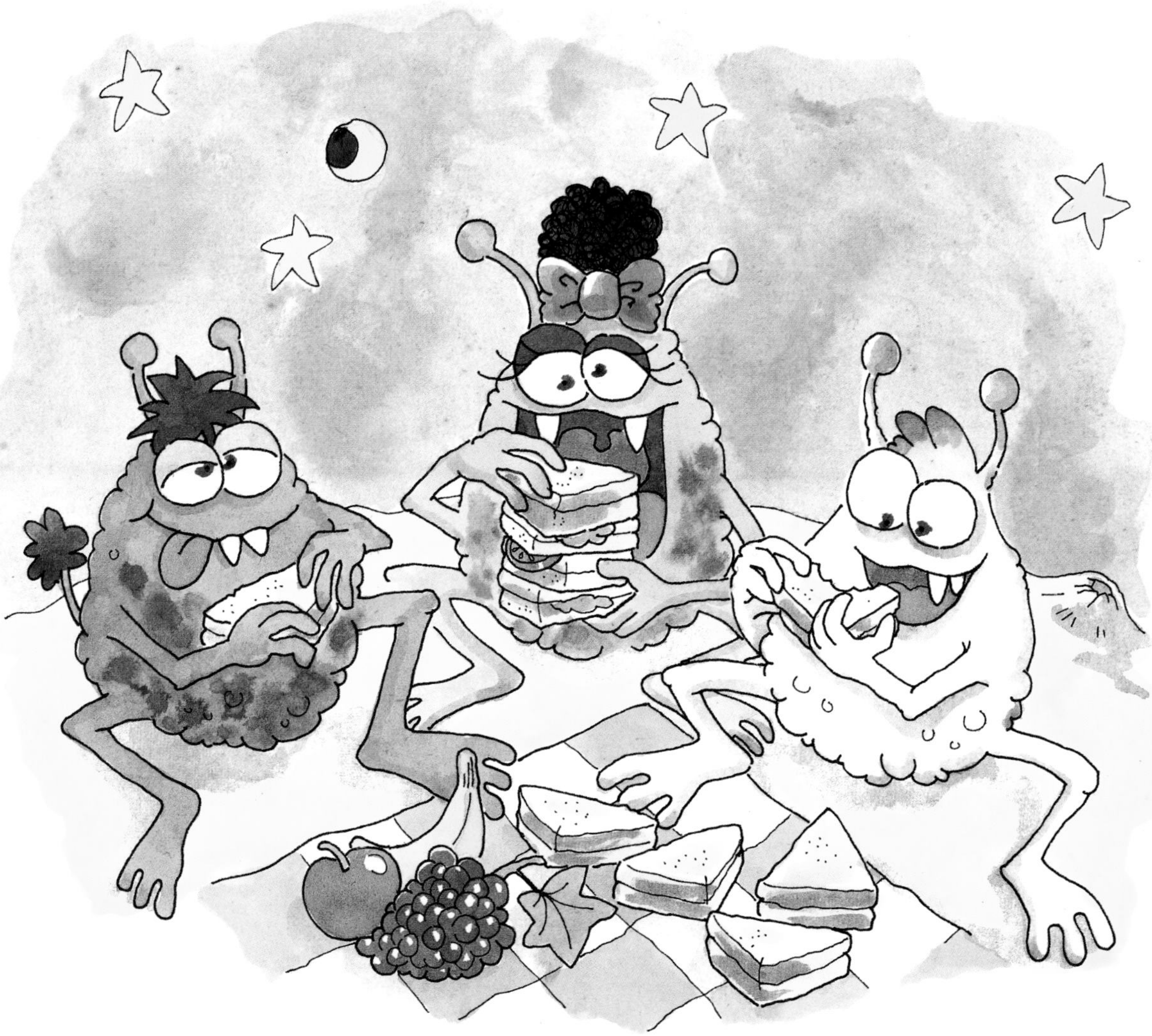

Gillian Hatch

Margaret Baker   Pat Cockett   Glenis Marriott

Nelson

Contents

Addition Quickies

You may need some number apparatus.

A

Look at this sum:

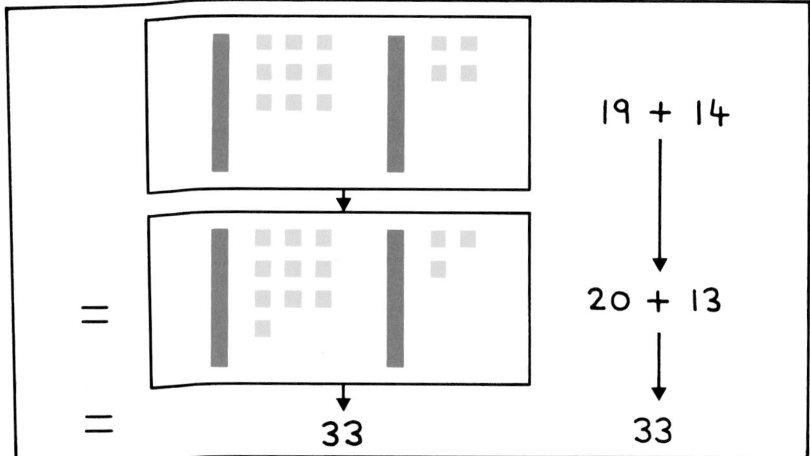

Can you find ways to do these?
The first sum is started for you.

1. 39 + 13
   = 40 + 12
   = ______
2. 29 + 16
3. 49 + 15
4. 39 + 12
5. 19 + 17
6. 59 + 14
7. 69 + 28
8. 79 + 13
9. 59 + 29
10. 29 + 21

B

Sometimes we change the numbers by 2, like this:

18 + 16
= 20 + 14
= 34

Try these.

1. 28 + 15
2. 28 + 14
3. 48 + 16
4. 38 + 17
5. 68 + 15
6. 38 + 18
7. 48 + 26
8. 38 + 25
9. 58 + 23

C

Now do these in the same way, but this time in your head
Write the answers only.

1. 48 + 13
2. 49 + 13
3. 59 + 12
4. 38 + 16
5. 69 + 25
6. 58 + 19
7. Invent 3 sums like these for a friend to do. Work out the answers.

D

Sometimes we have to decide which number to make up.

Sometimes we can see two ways of doing a sum.

Look out for the sums where you have to move 3 units!

Find two ways to do these. Write out how you do each way.

1. 18 + 19
2. 28 + 48
3. 39 + 18
4. 69 + 18
5. 38 + 59
6. 47 + 17
7. 28 + 67
8. 19 + 47
9. 68 + 37

A

Do you remember doing addition sums?
Copy and complete these.

1.
```
  916
  408
+ 796
-----
```

2.
```
  789
  685
+ 968
-----
```

3.
```
  876
  790
+ 629
-----
```

4.
```
  676
  769
+ 598
-----
```

Now try these.

5. 438 + 867 + 524
6. 849 + 983 + 935
7. 647 + 803 + 859
8. 789 + 625 + 846

B

Copy these and fill in the missing numbers.

1.
```
  5 3 6
+ 2 9 8
-------
  □ 3 □
```

2.
```
  5 8 □
+ □ 7 9
-------
  8 □ 9
```

3.
```
  □ 4 □
+ 3 6 7
-------
  8 □ 5
```

4.
```
  □ 2 9
  2 4 □
+ 1 □ 2
-------
  9 0 2
```

5.
```
  1 4 7
  3 1 □
+ □ 6 4
-------
  9 □ 1
```

6.
```
  □ □ □
+ □ □ □
-------
  8 4 7
```

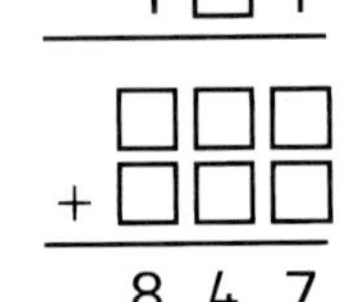

C

1. In February 432 books were borrowed from the school library. In March 497 were borrowed. How many books were borrowed altogether?
2. On a school holiday the children travelled 394km on the first day, 263km on the second day and 201km on the last day. How far did they travel altogether?
3. How many dinners does the cook make if 27 nursery children, 107 infants and 152 juniors stay for school dinner?
4. There were 904 books in the school library. Two parcels of new books arrived. There were 49 books in the first parcel and 57 books in the second parcel. How many books are there in the library now?

A

Here are Natalie's school library fines. Natalie has found a quick way to check that the librarian has added them up correctly. Look:

21 to the nearest ten is 20.
28 to the nearest ten is 30.
20 + 30 = 50.
So a 49p fine is about right.

We call this a check sum. It gives nearly the same answer.
Work out these sums. Check your answer with a check sum.

1. 29 + 42 = 71 — check sum 30 + 40 = 70
2. 19 + 32
3. 31 + 27
4. 51 + 29
5. 91 + 32
6. 89 + 22
7. 93 + 38
8. 98 + 91

B

When we work out the check sum for a number which ends in 5, we usually go up to the next ten.

For 55 + 42 the check sum is:

60 + 40
= 100

Now work out these sums and their check sums in your book.

1. 21 + 55
2. 72 + 95
3. 45 + 19
4. 58 + 45
5. 49 + 35

C

The check sum always gives an approximate answer. It's easy to work the check in our heads.

For 29 + 62 we write:

29 + 62 is approx. 90

Work out the approximate answers to these sums in your head. Then write them in your book.

1. 49 + 28 is approx. 80
2. 53 + 37
3. 47 + 28
4. 24 + 45
5. 47 + 92
6. 98 + 47
7. 101 + 39
8. 101 + 52

You may need a counting board and some number apparatus.

A

Try these sums.

You may need to change
1 ten for 10 units,
or 1 hundred for 10 tens,
or both.

1. 524 − 106 = ____
2. 653 − 228 = ____
3. 880 − 334 = ____
4. 782 − 213 = ____
5. 525 − 132 = ____
6. 756 − 160 = ____
7. 302 − 170 = ____
8. 519 − 351 = ____
9. 623 − 177 = ____
10. 810 − 356 = ____
11. 402 − 272 = ____
12. 925 − 149 = ____

B

Now try these problems.

1. The airport restaurant serves 624 people. 431 of them are adults. How many children are served?
2. On our flight to Italy there are 312 passengers. There are only 124 window seats. How many passengers will not be able to sit by a window?
3. The plane climbs 684 metres. At 950 metres it will be above the cloud level. How much further does it have to climb to get above the cloud level?
4. Subtract 470 from 832.
5. A plane holds 405 passengers. 297 seats are taken. How many seats are empty?

Counting Up

You may need a counting board and some number apparatus.

A

Try these. Be careful, you may need to exchange!

1. 804 − 639 = ____
2. 501 − 255 = ____
3. 502 − 287 = ____
4. 400 − 253 = ____
5. 602 − 125 = ____
6. 408 − 49 = ____
7. 402 − 356 = ____
8. 501 − 245 = ____
9. 708 − 409 = ____
10. 500 − 429 = ____

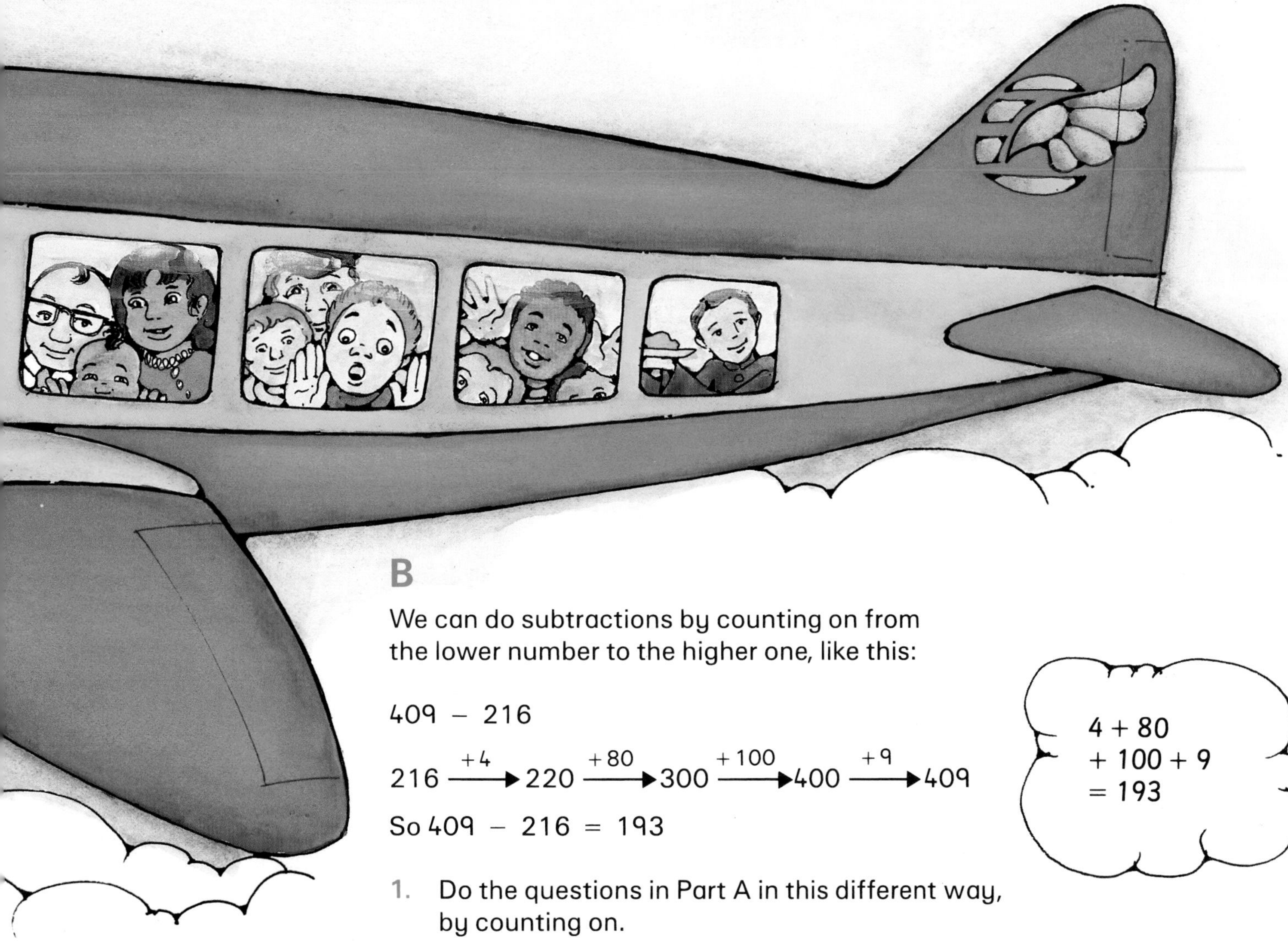

B

We can do subtractions by counting on from the lower number to the higher one, like this:

409 − 216

$216 \xrightarrow{+4} 220 \xrightarrow{+80} 300 \xrightarrow{+100} 400 \xrightarrow{+9} 409$

So 409 − 216 = 193

4 + 80
+ 100 + 9
= 193

1. Do the questions in Part A in this different way, by counting on.
2. Did you get the same answers?
3. Which way did you like best?

A

Look at this sum.

```
  3291
- 2196
  ----
  1095
```

It is like other subtractions,
but there are thousands in the numbers.

Try these.

1. 4162 − 1044
2. 8704 − 396
3. 2463 − 1246
4. 7720 − 4583
5. 8253 − 4136
6. 1673 − 205
7. 9876 − 3299
8. 2604 − 1068

B

Copy these sums and fill in the missing numbers.

1.
```
  4 8 1 □
- 2 □ 0 3
  -------
  2 7 1 4
```

2.
```
  9 9 2 7
- 5 □ □ 2
  -------
  4 2 6 5
```

3.
```
  5 1 7 □
- 3 □ 4 8
  -------
  □ 1 2 6
```

4.
```
  □ 6 1 7
- 5 1 □ □
  -------
  4 4 5 3
```

C

Copy out these puzzle sentences, and fill in the spaces with some sensible figures.
Then work out the answers.

1. The travel agent sells 4907 holidays a year. There are ________ holidays in Europe. How many are holidays outside Europe?
2. 5973 passengers arrived at London airport. ________ of them spoke English. How many did not speak English?
3. The plane has flown 6952 kilometres. It flew ________ kilometres over the land. How many kilometres did it fly over the sea?
4. The school secretary sends 2983 letters a year. Out of these ________ are to people abroad. How many are to people in this country?

Monster Multiplication 6 ■ 3

 You will need the worksheet called Machine Records.

A Here are two multiplication machines.

Fill in a table like this for each machine.

In	Out
25	
29	
34	
19	
24	
55	

B

Roary, Yell, Strum, Rap, Heavy and Rocky are all members of a monster pop group. The name of their group is hidden in these sums.

1. Copy and complete the sum for each letter.

T	9 × 21	U	2 × 71	H	5 × 17	M	3 × 47	S	7 × 99
R	8 × 72	L	5 × 37	E	6 × 93	I	4 × 53	L	6 × 62
T	3 × 28	I	7 × 73	E	2 × 43	P	4 × 86		

2. Put the answers in order, smallest first.
3. Write the correct letter underneath each answer to find the pop group's name.

   It starts: T H _   _ _ _ _ _ _ _ _ _ _ _ _

C

1. The group practises for 26 hours a week. How many hours do they practise in 5 weeks?
2. Gruff saves 65p a week towards a new album. How much money will he save in 8 weeks?
3. The group's fan club are going to a pop concert. Each coach holds 49 fans and 3 coaches are needed. How many fans are going to the concert if all the coaches are full?

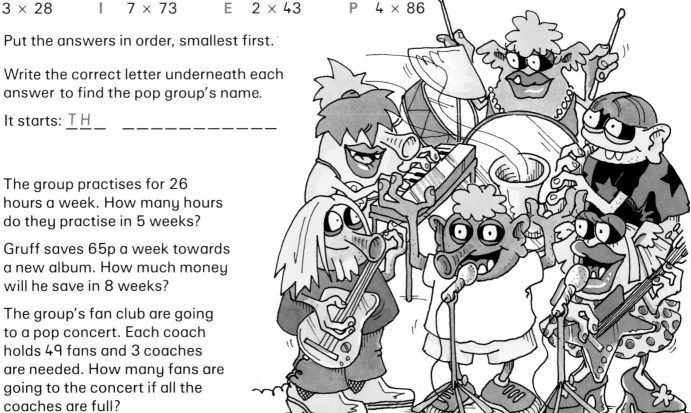

Multiplication With Hundreds

A

 You will need some counting boards and number apparatus.

The Multipliers need to practise their multiplication as well as their music.
A counting board can help them with their sums.
Strum worked out 3 × 267 on counting boards, like this:

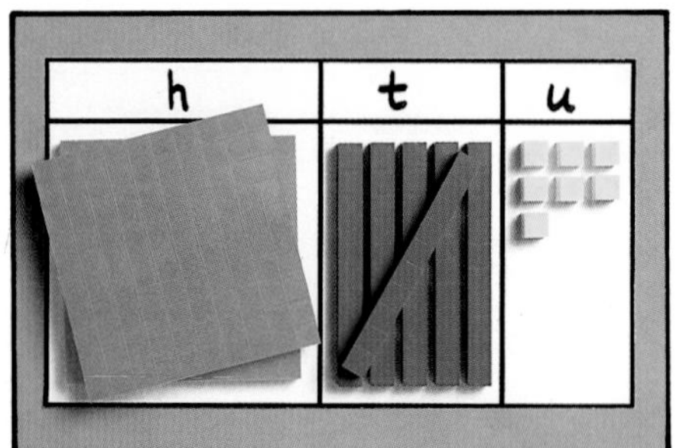

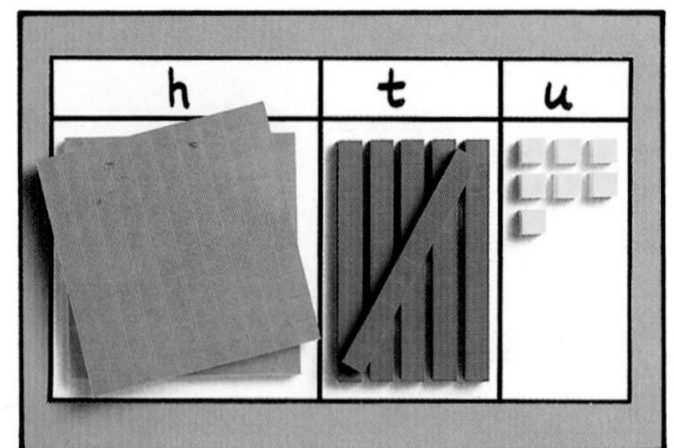

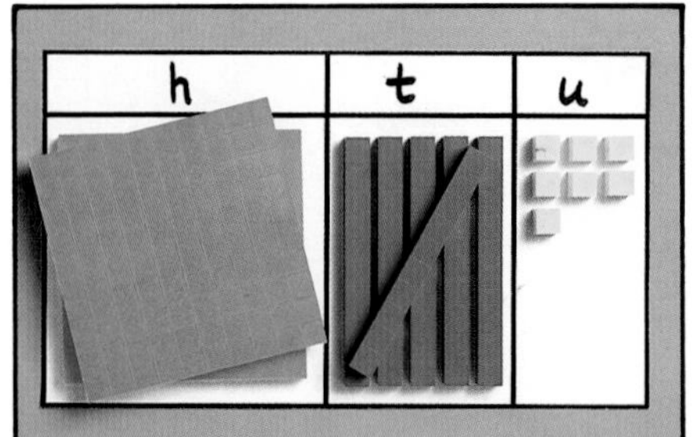

She wrote: $3 \times 267 = 3 \times 2h + 3 \times 6t + 3 \times 7u$
$= 6h + 18t + 21u$ ← Tidy up the units.
$= 6h + 20t + 1u$ ← Tidy up the tens.
$= 8h + 0t + 1u$
$= 801$

Now do these on your counting boards.

1. 3 × 134
2. 2 × 156
3. 3 × 238
4. 2 × 129
5. 3 × 147
6. 2 × 165
7. 3 × 313
8. 3 × 308
9. 2 × 275

B

Yell can do these without counting boards.
See if you can do them without counting boards too.

1. 2 × 473
2. 3 × 264
3. 2 × 397
4. 2 × 409
5. 3 × 235
6. 2 × 286
7. 3 × 199
8. 3 × 208

Now do these the way you like best.

9. 2 × 390
10. 3 × 256
11. 2 × 367
12. 3 × 144
13. 3 × 285
14. 2 × 359
15. 2 × 468
16. 3 × 107

C

1. Match the questions and the answers.

Questions

3 × 147 3 × 254
2 × 191 2 × 173
3 × 322 2 × 496

Answers

966 382
346 762
441 992

2. Now use a calculator to check your answers.

A

Roberta had a useful computer program.
When she typed in

3, 8, 24

the computer understood $3 \times 8 = 24$.

It told her two division sentences

$24 \div 8 = 3$
$24 \div 3 = 8$

For each of these pairs of numbers find the third number Roberta must type in.
Then write what the computer screen will tell her.

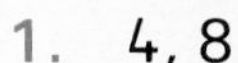

1. 4, 8
2. 5, 9
3. 7, 8
4. 4, 9
5. 9, 3
6. 7, 9
7. 6, 8
8. 8, 9
9. 5, 8
10. 6, 9
11. 8, 8
12. 9, 9

B

Roberta also had a secret code with her friend Sally.
They could only use eleven coded letters, but they used ordinary letters for the others.
Their code was:

TOP SECRET
A E H I M N O S T U Y
0 1 2 3 4 5 6 7 8 9 10

To get each of the numbers they wrote a division sum.
So to code HELLO they could use:

$(16 \div 8)\ (9 \div 9)$ LL $(54 \div 9)$

Decode these.

1. $(56 \div 8)\ (8 \div 8)\ (9 \div 9)$ $(90 \div 9)\ (48 \div 8)\ (72 \div 8)$ $(63 \div 9)\ (54 \div 9)\ (48 \div 8)\ (40 \div 8)$
2. $(36 \div 9)\ (80 \div 8)$ $(45 \div 9)\ (0 \div 8)\ (32 \div 8)\ (8 \div 8)$ $(24 \div 8)\ (56 \div 8)$
   $(63 \div 9)\ (0 \div 9)$ L L $(90 \div 9)$
3. Now put your own message into code. Exchange messages with your friend and decode.
   Were both messages right?

A

You will need the worksheet called Machine Records.

Look at this machine.

1. Fill in a table for this machine.

In	Middle	Out
16		
24		
32		
8		
40		
56		
48		
72		
64		
80		

2. What single machine would do the same job? Fill in a table to show that it works for all the numbers.

B

On Friday Hamish's class visit the fruit farm.

1. What is the cost of 1 apple?
2. What is the cost of 1 pear?
3. Teacher wants 24 apples to make toffee apples for the bonfire party. How many bags must she buy?
4. Mr Taylor wants 36 pears. How many bags must he buy?
5. Miss Baker wants 60 pears for her shop. How many bags must she buy?
6. The school kitchen needs 62 apples and 58 pears. How many bags of each must they buy?
7. I want to buy exactly 100 fruits. Is there a way to do it?

At The Theme Park

A

Work out all these sharing divisions.

1. 84 ÷ 7	5. 90 ÷ 6	9. 75 ÷ 4	13. 82 ÷ 8
2. 99 ÷ 9	6. 96 ÷ 4	10. 94 ÷ 7	14. 89 ÷ 7
3. 96 ÷ 8	7. 95 ÷ 8	11. 79 ÷ 5	15. 80 ÷ 6
4. 76 ÷ 6	8. 91 ÷ 6	12. 97 ÷ 9	16. 99 ÷ 7

17. Choose two of the sums and write a story about them.

B

1. 84 children went to the theme park. There were 3 coaches. An equal number travelled on each coach. How many children on each coach?
2. The children were divided into 7 equal groups to go round the theme park. How many in each group?
3. The total cost for them all was £91. How much did it cost for each group?
4. Annie and her 8 friends bought a large bag of sweets. There were 96 sweets in the bag. How many sweets did they each get? How many were left over?
5. Asif and his 7 friends won 93p. How much did they each win? How much was left over?
6. The teachers brought 81 packs of sandwiches. How many for each group? How many packets were left over for the teachers?
7. A group of 6 children won 85 free tokens. It costs 15 tokens for half an hour in the Moon Walk. Can all 6 children have a turn?

A

1. How many groups of 5 can you make from 85?
   Work it out carefully. Record in the way you like best.

Now work these out in the same way.

2. 64 ÷ 4
3. 84 ÷ 6
4. 75 ÷ 5
5. 91 ÷ 7
6. 99 ÷ 9
7. 96 ÷ 8
8. 92 ÷ 4
9. 93 ÷ 8
10. 97 ÷ 5
11. 93 ÷ 9
12. 95 ÷ 6
13. 91 ÷ 8
14. Write a story for two of these sums.

B

1. Caramels are packed 8 to a bag. How many bags can be filled with 75 caramels?
2. Chocolates are packed 9 to a box. How many boxes can be filled with 97 chocolates?
3. Moon bars are packed in fours. How many packs can be made with 75 bars?
4. There are 98 mint creams to be packed into sixes. How many packs can be made?
5. 70 chocolate mice are ready to be packed. They could be packed in threes or in fours. Which would leave fewer mice unpacked?
6. 96 fudge pieces are packed in bags of 8. They sell the bags at 10p each. How much money do they get?

A

Katy was given a calculator for her birthday. Now she says it's her best friend!
She can even make it say 'hello'. (Press .1134 and turn the calculator upside down.)

Now find the button which clears your calculator. Press it.
Now press 1753 + 8246 =
Did you get 9999? If not, try again.

Work these out on your calculator.

1. 8 + 6
2. 6 + 8
3. 13 + 17
4. 17 + 13
5. 86 + 93
6. 93 + 86
7. 273 + 159
8. 159 + 273
9. 854 + 962
10. 962 + 854
11. 627 + 579
12. 579 + 627
13. 1729 + 4336
14. 4336 + 1729
15. 3021 + 5068
16. 5068 + 3021
17. What do you notice about the answers? Write about it in your book.

B

This time you are going to guess first.
For each sum, write down what you think the answer is.
Then do the sum on the calculator.

1. 499 + 1
2. 2399 + 1
3. 2999 + 1
4. 1099 + 1
5. 6999 + 1
6. 7999 + 1
7. 5999 + 1
8. 3399 + 1
9. 9909 + 1
10. 9009 + 1
11. 9099 + 1
12. 9999 + 1

C

Now try these.
Guess first each time, and then do each sum on the calculator.

1. 990 + 10
2. 390 + 10
3. 2390 + 10
4. 4870 + 10
5. 2990 + 10
6. 4990 + 10
7. 4190 + 10
8. 9980 + 10
9. 1265 + 10
10. 3900 + 100
11. 3917 + 100
12. 3927 + 100

A

The calculator has a [−] button for subtraction.
Work these out.

1. 7 − 4 = 3
2. 18 − 15
3. 91 − 27
4. 94 − 30
5. 87 − 56
6. 89 − 58
7. 156 − 103
8. 168 − 115
9. 799 − 460
10. 802 − 463

B

Do these in your head. Write down the answer. Check it on your calculator.

1. 300 − 1
2. 300 − 10
3. 800 − 1
4. 800 − 10
5. 890 − 1
6. 1000 − 10
7. 2000 − 1
8. 3900 − 10
9. 3900 − 1
10. 5000 − 10

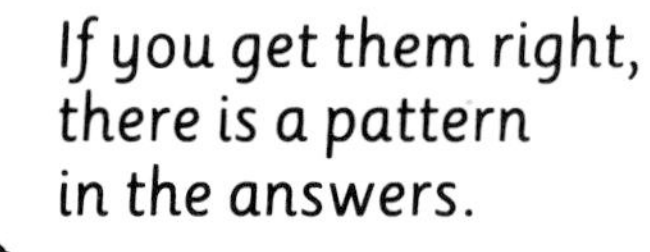

If you get them right, there is a pattern in the answers.

Did you get back to where you started?

C

Check this on your calculator: 583 − 139 = 444
Now work out: 444 + 139 = ?
You should get back to 583.

Now do these. Write down the answer to the subtraction. Then add, as above, to check the sum.

1. 324 − 193
2. 765 − 264
3. 357 − 168
4. 622 − 491
5. 456 − 62
6. 601 − 257
7. 999 − 669

D

Use your calculator to find out what number goes in the box. You can only use the [+] button not the [−] one.

1. 563 − □ = 560
2. 563 − □ = 503
3. 563 − □ = 63
4. 1376 − □ = 1370
5. 1376 − □ = 1306
6. 1376 − □ = 1076
7. 1376 − □ = 376
8. 5974 − □ = 5074

A

Do you remember how we worked out check sums in Topic 1?
Here's one: 18 + 42 is approximately 20 + 40, so the answer is about 60.
We can do this with three numbers too: 18 + 42 + 59 is approximately 20 + 40 + 60, so the answer is about 120.

Try these sums to give you practice in adding up tens in your head.
Just write the answers.

1. 90 + 20
2. 40 + 30
3. 50 + 80 + 30
4. 70 + 30 + 20
5. 90 + 60 + 90
6. 50 + 80 + 60
7. 90 + 30 + 20
8. 40 + 20 + 50

B

We can use this adding in tens to check that we have used the calculator correctly.

We want to work out 29 + 47 + 71. The calculator gets 147.
Did we press the right buttons? To check, you must do the approximate sum. So 30 + 50 + 70 = 150.
The answers are nearly the same. If they had not been nearly the same you would know you had pressed the wrong buttons.

Do each of these sums on the calculator and write down the answer.
Then do its check sum and write down the approximate answer.

1. 48 + 37 + 54 = 139 (Check 50 + 40 + 50 = 140)
2. 43 + 67 + 22
3. 38 + 52 + 74
4. 87 + 39 + 52
5. 91 + 72 + 31
6. 76 + 82 + 61
7. 89 + 89 + 98
8. 91 + 43 + 57
9. 56 + 97 + 28
10. 98 + 19 + 53
11. 24 + 86 + 65
12. 99 + 99 + 99

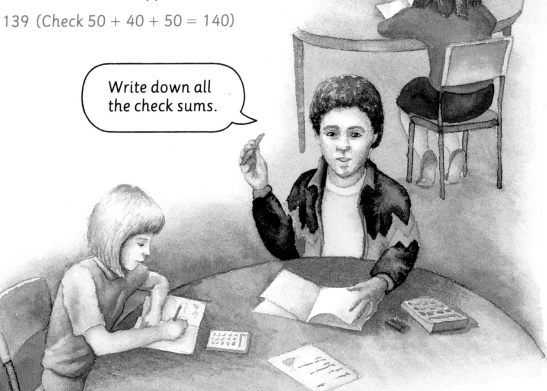

Write down all the check sums.

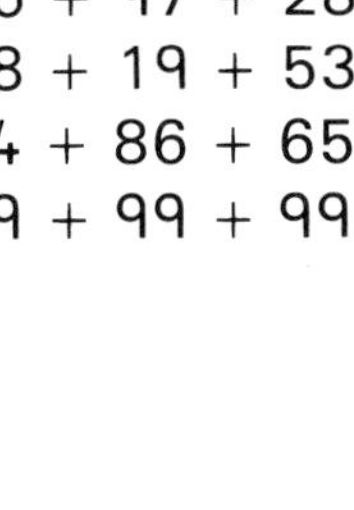

Brackets Galore! 6 5

A

Work with a friend on this page.
There are two sums in each question.
One of you should do the first sum each time.
One of you should do the second sum each time.

Remember, brackets mean 'do this part first'.

1. (1729 + 452) + 167
   1729 + (452 + 167)

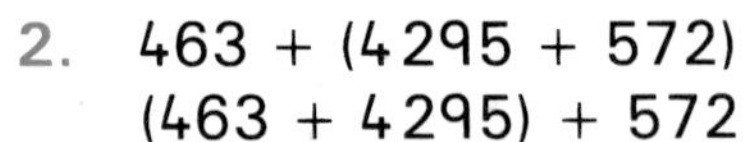
Did you get the same answer?

2. 463 + (4295 + 572)
   (463 + 4295) + 572
3. (5163 + 2164) + 1092
   5163 + (2164 + 1092)
4. 2176 + (4819 + 1999)
   (2176 + 4819) + 1999
5. (3876 + 2095) + 4765
   3876 + (2095 + 4765)
6. Write about any pattern you see.

B

Now try some subtractions.
Work in the same way.

1. 963 − (526 − 179)
   (963 − 526) − 179
2. (1935 − 872) − 361
   1935 − (872 − 361)
3. 8765 − (1234 − 1029)
   (8765 − 1234) − 1029
4. (7138 − 6943) − 195
   7138 − (6943 − 195)
5. 8000 − (7000 − 1)
   (8000 − 7000) − 1
6. Write about what happens this time.

C

Now try these.
Look carefully at the + and − signs.

1. (816 + 245) − 169
   816 + (245 − 169)
2. 1836 − (762 + 326)
   (1836 − 762) + 326
3. (3723 − 1091) + 618
   3723 − (1091 + 618)
4. 8152 + (1976 − 1235)
   (8152 + 1976) − 1235
5. (7983 − 4762) + 1290
   7983 − (4762 + 1290)
6. Can you explain when the answers are the same?
   When are they different?

A

You will need Ivor's machine, some number cards and some sign cards.
Work with a friend.

Use Ivor's machine to work out each of these pairs of sums.

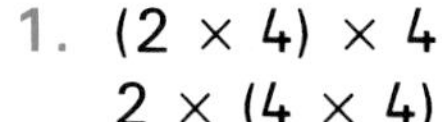

1. $(2 \times 4) \times 4$
   $2 \times (4 \times 4)$
2. $(5 \times 2) \times 10$
   $5 \times (2 \times 10)$
3. $(2 \times 3) \times 7$
   $2 \times (3 \times 7)$
4. $(2 \times 5) \times 6$
   $2 \times (5 \times 6)$
5. $(3 \times 3) \times 8$
   $3 \times (3 \times 8)$
6. $(2 \times 2) \times 10$
   $2 \times (2 \times 10)$

Write them
like this:
(2 × 4) × 4
↓
8 × 4

B

Now try these in the same way.

1. $(40 \div 4) \div 2$
   $40 \div (4 \div 2)$
2. $(12 \div 2) \div 2$
   $12 \div (2 \div 2)$
3. $(24 \div 4) \div 2$
   $24 \div (4 \div 2)$
4. $(48 \div 6) \div 2$
   $48 \div (6 \div 2)$
5. $(60 \div 6) \div 2$
   $60 \div (6 \div 2)$
6. $(72 \div 4) \div 2$
   $72 \div (4 \div 2)$

C

You will need a calculator.

Ivor decided to use both kinds of machine together. Work out these for him.

1. $(48 \div 8) \times 2$
   $48 \div (8 \times 2)$
2. $(10 \times 4) \div 2$
   $10 \times (4 \div 2)$
3. $(60 \div 6) \times 2$
   $60 \div (6 \times 2)$
4. $(8 \times 6) \div 3$
   $8 \times (6 \div 3)$
5. $(72 \div 6) \times 3$
   $72 \div (6 \times 3)$
6. $(150 \div 10) \times 5$
   $150 \div (10 \times 5)$

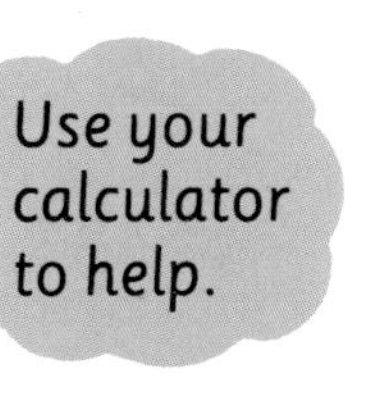
Use your
calculator
to help.

Faster Machines

You will need the worksheet called Machine Records.

A

1. Here is a double division machine.
   Fill in a table for it.

In	Middle	Out
24	8	4
12		
30		
60		
96		

2. This single machine does the same job
   but much faster! Fill in a table for it.

In	Out
24	4
12	
30	
60	
96	

So ÷ 6
is the same as
÷ 3 then ÷ 2.

B

1. Here is another double division machine.
   Fill in a table for it.

In	Middle	Out
8		
12		
16		
20		
24		

2. What single machine will do the same job?
   Talk to your teacher about it.

   Think about your tables.

3. Put these numbers into the double machine. Write down what comes out.
   (a) 64 (b) 48 (c) 56 (d) 84 (e) 72 (f) 96

4. Put the same numbers into your single machine.
   Write down what comes out. Do you get the same answers?

More End Digits

You will need the worksheet called Machine Records.

A

Here is an end-digit machine.
It multiplies by 5.

1. Fill in a table like this:

In	Out
1	5
2	
3	

Continue the table up to 10.

2. Write about the pattern in the numbers printed by the machine.
   What would the machine print if we put in the next 10 numbers?
3. Now write out the table of fives.
   Continue up to 20 × 5.
   Can you see the same pattern?

B

You will need a calculator.

Here is a divide by 5 machine.

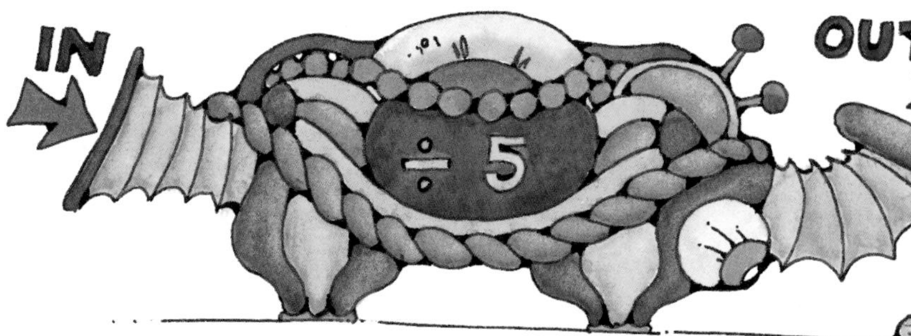

1. Put all the numbers from 20 to 30 into the machine.
   Fill in a table to show your results.
2. Which numbers in question 1 divided exactly by 5?
3. How can you tell whether a number can be divided exactly by 5?
4. Which of these numbers can be divided exactly by 5?
   Write them in your book.

17	37	65	80	91
22	45	67	84	92
25	50	72	87	95
36	52	75	90	100

A

Here is another end-digit machine.
When 5 goes in, 0 comes out.

1. Put some other numbers into the machine.
   What does the machine keep on printing?
2. How can we tell if a number is a multiple of 10?
3. Which of these numbers can be divided exactly by 10? Write them down.

   40 74 80 95 100 150 213 330 460 585 690 710

B

Look at this set of numbers.

9 14 20 21 25 32 40 47 55 59 66 70 75 80 89

1. Copy this diagram and fill it in using these numbers.

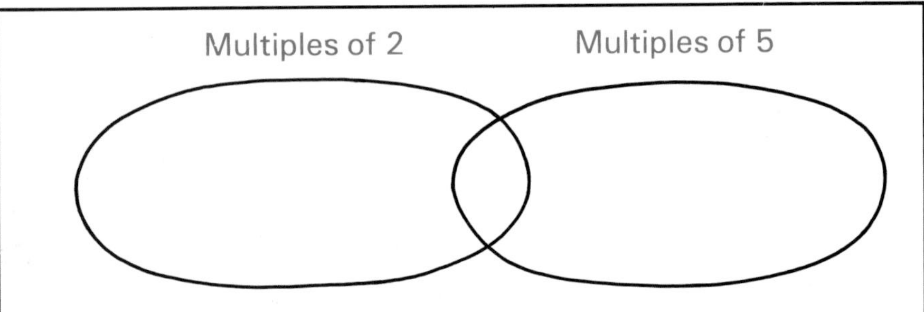

2. What do you notice about the numbers which belong to both sets?

C

 You will need the worksheet called Machine Records.

Here are two more end-digit machines.

1. Fill in a table for each machine.
2. Write about the ways in which the patterns are the same.
3. Write about the ways in which the patterns are different.

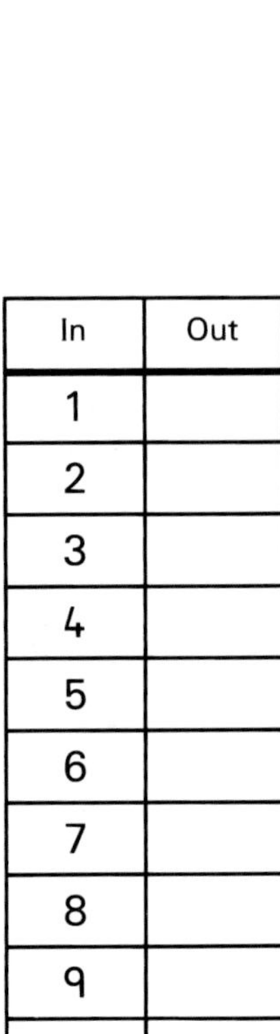

In	Out
1	
2	
3	
4	
5	
6	
7	
8	
9	
10	

You will need the worksheet called Machine Records.

This special machine makes one-digit numbers.
If you put in 8, the machine prints 8.
If you put in 27, the machine works out 2 + 7 and prints 9.
If you put in 47, the machine works out 4 + 7 = 11 and then 1 + 1 = 2.

1. Work out what the machine does to each of these numbers.

(a) 12 (c) 63 (e) 463
(b) 34 (d) 125 (f) 896

2. Put the numbers from the table of threes into the machine.
Fill in a table like this.

In	Out
3	
6	
9	
12	
15	
30	

3. Write about the pattern.

4. Do the same for the numbers from the table of nines.

9 18 27 36 45 54 63 72 81 90

Coconut Shy

Graph showing children's scores

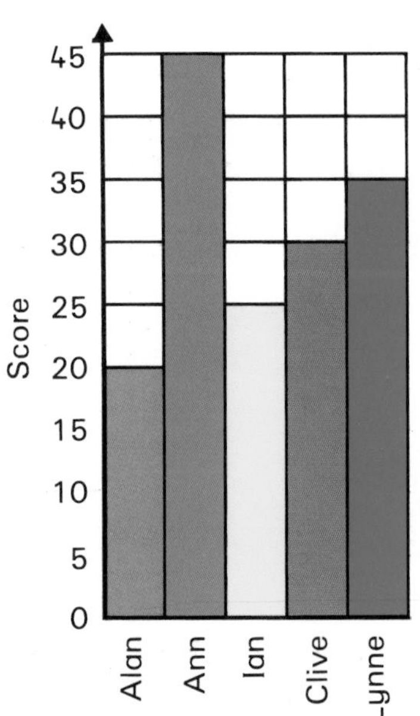

A

Here is a graph showing five children's scores on the Coconut Shy. Use it to answer these questions.

1. How many does each step on the score axis represent?
2. Write down the score for each child.
3. Now write down the children's names in order, starting with the winner.
4. How many more did Clive score than Alan?
5. How many did the two girls score together?
6. How many did the three boys score together?
7. What was the difference between the highest score and the lowest score?

B

Now look at this graph.

1. (a) How many does each step on the score axis represent?
   (b) How many does half a step represent?
2. Now answer questions 2 to 7 in Part A using this new graph.
8. What do you notice?
9. Try to explain why this happened.

Graph showing children's scores

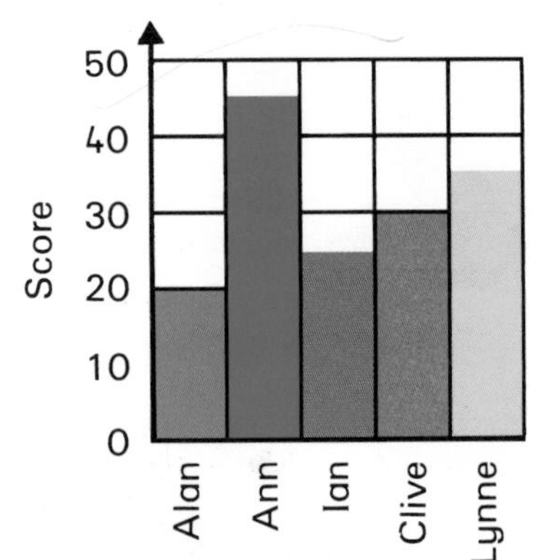

You will need a dice marked 1–6, some squared paper, a ruler and some coloured pencils.

A

John threw a dice 50 times.
He recorded his results like this:

Number on dice	Number of times thrown
1	卌 卌 ||
2	卌 |||
3	卌 ||||
4	卌 卌
5	卌 |
6	卌

1. Make a table for him like this:

Number on dice	Number of times thrown
1	12
2	
3	
4	
5	
6	

2. John made a graph of his results. Copy and complete his graph on squared paper.

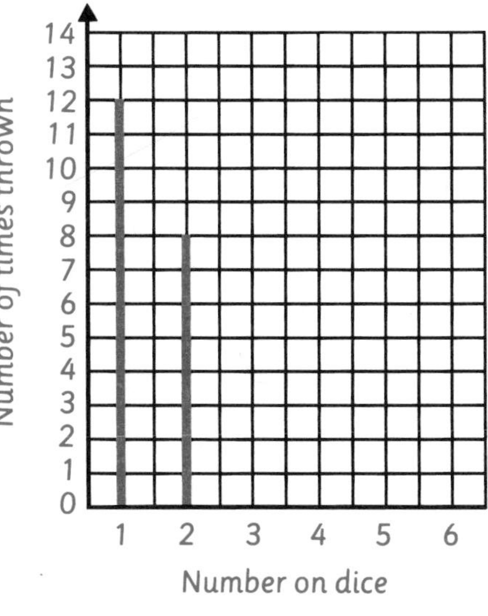

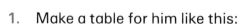

B

1. Get a dice. Throw it 50 times. Record your results like John did. Make a graph to show your results.
2. Now add your scores to John's scores. Draw the new graph.

You may need to use a different scale.

C

John got bored throwing the dice. He wrote a computer program to throw it for him. It did 500 throws.

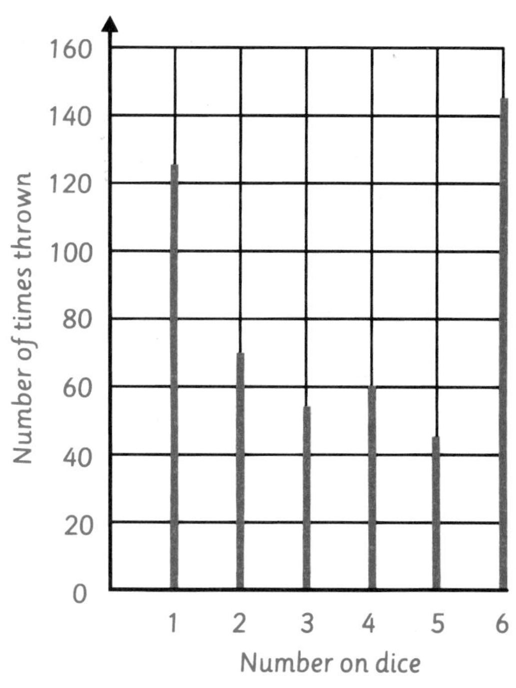

1. Write down how many of each number the computer threw.
2. Do you think the computer did a good job? Why?

You will need some squared paper, a ruler and a seconds timer.

A

This bar-line graph shows the number of customers each of five fairground stalls had in one hour.

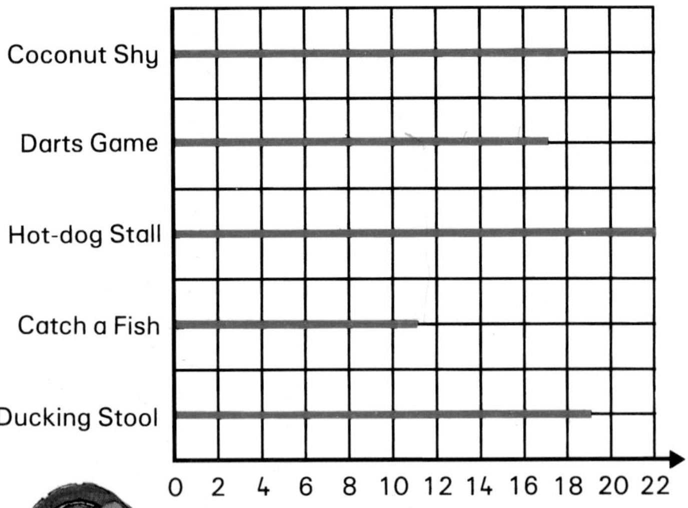

1. What does each step on the horizontal axis represent?
2. Which stall had the most customers?
3. Which stall had the fewest customers?
4. How many more customers did the Darts Game have than Catch a Fish?
5. How many more customers did the Ducking Stool have than the Coconut Shy?
6. Here is a list showing how many customers each stall had in the last hour.

Coconut Shy	28	Catch a Fish	15
Darts Game	16	Ducking Stool	26
Hot-dog Stall	19		

Make a bar-line graph to show the number of customers at each stall in the last hour.

B

Six children wrote their names five times and timed how long it took.
Look at the graph they drew.

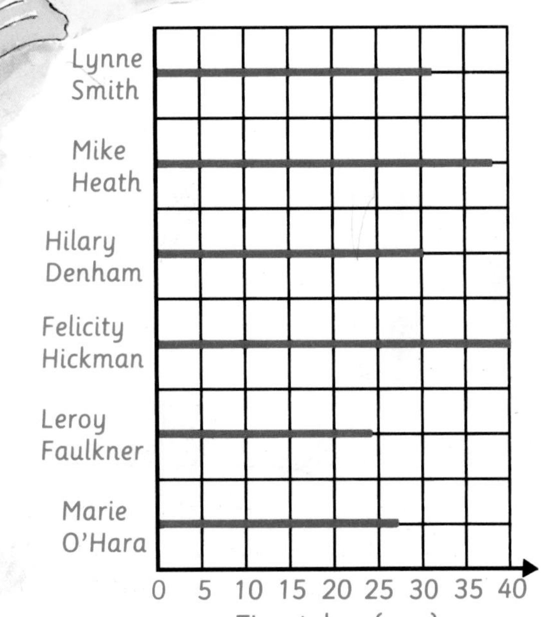

1. What does each step on the horizontal axis represent?
2. How long did the quickest person take? Who was it?
3. How long did the slowest person take? Who was it?
4. Which two people took nearly the same time?
5. Now time yourself and 5 of your friends writing their names 5 times. Draw a graph of your results.
6. Put the times in order starting with the shortest.
7. Put your names in order of length starting with the shortest.
8. Are the orders the same?

Fair Shares

A

You may need some coins.

We want to share £9·14 equally between 2 people.

£9·14 ÷ 2

To work out the sum we write it down like this:

 £4 · 5 7
2 | £9 · ^{1}1^{1}4

Now do these in the same way.
Use coins to help if you like.

1. Share £5·48 equally between 2 people.
2. Share £10·56 equally between 3 people.
3. Share £9·68 equally between 4 people.
4. Share £6·55 equally between 5 people.
5. Share £8·54 equally between 2 people.
6. Share £10·74 equally between 3 people.
7. Share £14·16 equally between 4 people.
8. Share £17·85 equally between 5 people.

B

Sometimes we have to take special care.

£5·25 ÷ 5

We write it like this:

 £1 ·
5 | £5 · 2 5

This time there are not enough tenpence pieces to share. We change the 2 tenpence pieces into 20 pennies. We write:

 £1 · 0
5 | £5 · 2^{2}5

Don't forget to say there are no tenpence pieces in the answer.

Now it's easy.

 £1 · 0 5
5 | £5 · 2^{2}5

Try these.

1. £8·18 ÷ 2
2. £9·24 ÷ 3
3. £12·16 ÷ 4
4. £4·36 ÷ 4
5. £20·45 ÷ 5
6. £32·48 ÷ 8
7. £14·35 ÷ 7
8. £18·72 ÷ 9
9. £3·42 ÷ 6
10. £7·29 ÷ 9

C

1. Jane travels to work by bus, 6 days a week. It costs her £8·64 a week. How much a day is this?
2. 3 packets of frozen pizzas cost £4·74. What does one packet cost?
3. 7 children went on a train journey. The fares came to £8·68. How much was each child's fare?
4. A pack of 6 blank video cassettes cost £12·54. How much does each cassette cost?
5. 7 boxes of chocolate truffles cost £13·37. What would I pay for 1 box?
6. Mr Barker bought a newspaper every day for a week. They were all the same price. He spent £3·15. How much did each newspaper cost?

Oranges And Lemons

A

How many oranges can be bought with £1·35?

Set it out like this:

£1·35		
– £0·90	⟵	10 oranges at 9p
£0·45		
– £0·45	⟵	5 oranges at 9p
£0·00		15 altogether

So 15 oranges can be bought with £1·35.

Do these the same way.

1. How many lemons can be bought with £1·19?
2. How many apples can be bought with £1·51?
3. How many peaches can be bought with £1·26?
4. How many pears can be bought with £1·46?
5. How many apricots can be bought with £1·22?
6. How many oranges can be bought with £1·62?

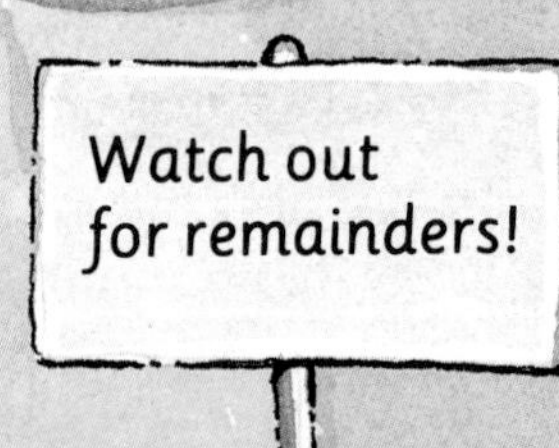

B

Sometimes we can buy more than one lot of 10.
Try these.

1. How many plums can be bought with £1·44?
2. How many lemons can be bought with £1·54?
3. How many oranges can be bought with £1·89?
4. How many apples can be bought with £1·86?
5. How many peaches can be bought with £2?

C

Answer Yes or No and explain why.

1. Can I buy 20 lemons with £1·30?
2. Can I buy 15 oranges with £1·50?
3. Can I buy 17 apples with £1·36?
4. Can I buy 30 plums with £1·75?
5. Can I buy 26 bananas with £2·60?
6. Can I buy 33 grapefruits with £6·60?

Work with a friend.
Which is the best offer in each question? Show in your book how you found out.

9. Look at question 8 again. Write down a reason why you might make the more expensive choice.

10. Now do the same for questions 1 to 7.

A

You will need a ruler marked in centimetres and millimetres.

Rosie is making a model windmill for the school garden.
She needs to measure a piece of wood.
Her ruler has centimetres marked on it.

The piece of wood is between 9cm and 10cm long.

Rosie measures the piece of wood again.
This time she uses a ruler with centimetres and millimetres marked on it.

The piece of wood is 9 centimetres and 6 millimetres long.
Rosie writes: 9cm 6mm

1. Look at your ruler carefully. How many millimetres are there in one centimetre? Remember to write cm for centimetres and mm for millimetres.
2. Copy and complete this table using your own measurements.

Object	cm and mm
Length of my pencil	___ cm ___ mm
Thickness of my pencil	
Width of my library book	
Thickness of my library book	
Length of my middle finger	

3. Which was the shortest measurement? Which was the longest?

B

Look at this ruler.

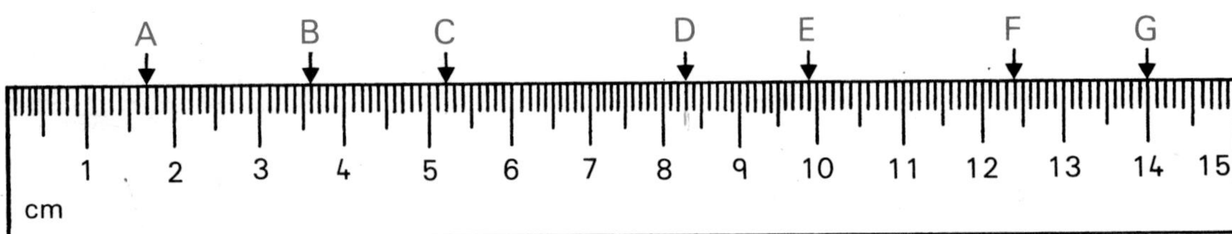

A points to 1cm 7mm or 1·7cm.

Copy and complete these in the same way.

1. B points to ______
2. C points to ______
3. D points to ______
4. E points to ______
5. F points to ______
6. G points to ______

A

The school garden is 15 metres and 32 centimetres long.
We can write: 15m 32cm or 15·32m
Write these both ways.

1. 6 metres and 72 centimetres
2. 10 metres and 35 centimetres
3. 17 metres and 83 centimetres
4. 18 metres and 51 centimetres
5. 15 metres and 6 centimetres
6. 2 metres and 7 centimetres

B

Rani and Laura are weeding the garden.
They have weeded three rows.
Each row measures 3·21 metres.

That makes

$$\begin{array}{r} 3\cdot21\text{m} \\ \times \quad 3 \\ \hline 9\cdot63\text{m} \\ \hline \end{array}$$

We have weeded a total of 9·63m.

Now do these.

1. 4 × 4·21m
2. 5 × 2·10m
3. 3 × 5·32m
4. 2 × 1·44m
5. 6 × 11·10m
6. 7 × 5·01m

C

Scott and Tamara are making bird scarers from silver paper and lengths of string.
They need to protect four rows of seeds each measuring 2m 41cm.
How much string do they need altogether?

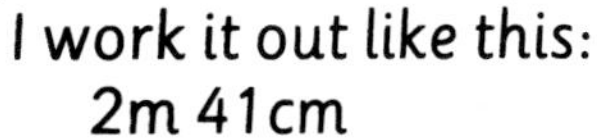

I work it out like this:

$$\begin{array}{r} 2\text{m } 41\text{cm} \\ \times \quad\quad 4 \\ \hline 9\text{m } 64\text{cm} \\ \hline {\scriptstyle 1\text{m}} \end{array}$$

I changed 164cm to 1m 64cm in the middle.

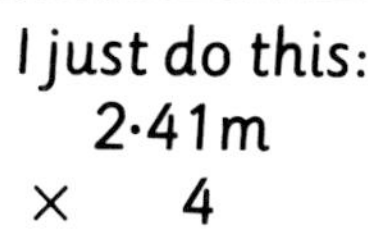

I just do this:

$$\begin{array}{r} 2\cdot41\text{m} \\ \times \quad 4 \\ \hline 9\cdot64\text{m} \\ \hline {\scriptstyle 1} \end{array}$$

It's quicker, and a lot easier if there is more than one exchange.

Now work these out.
Do the first three Scott's way.
Then try Tamara's way for questions 4 to 9.

1. 5 × 2m 31cm
2. 4 × 3m 32cm
3. 6 × 8m 27cm
4. 3 × 10·42m
5. 4 × 12·30m
6. 3 × 8·46m
7. 4 × 3·33m
8. 5 × 8·50m
9. 3 × 2·39m

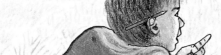

A

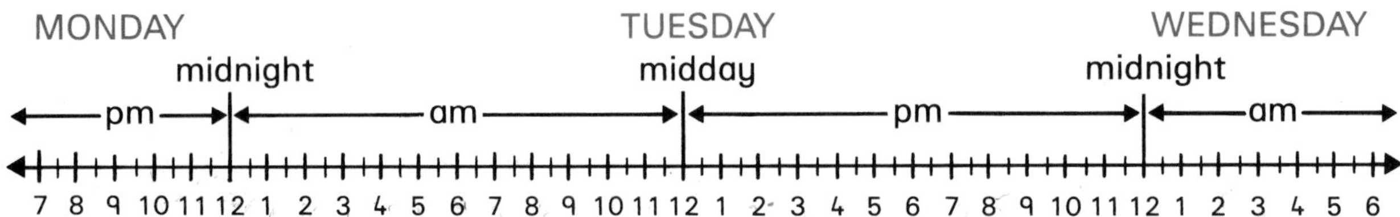

Use the line to find the time 9 hours after:

1. 2am Tuesday
2. 9pm Monday
3. 4pm Tuesday
4. 10am Tuesday

Use the line to find how long it is between:

5. 9pm Monday and 6am Tuesday
6. 7.30pm Tuesday and 2am Wednesday
7. midnight Monday and 8pm Tuesday
8. 9.30pm Monday and 6am Tuesday

B

How long is it from 8.15am to 1.05pm?
Look at this:

8.15am —45 mins→ 9am —3 hrs→ 12 noon —1 hr→ 1pm —5 mins→ 1.05pm

Total time is 4 hours 50 minutes

Do these in the same way.

1. 9.35am to 2.30pm
2. 7.40pm to 5.25am
3. 9.20am to 6.35pm
4. 5.35pm to 1.40am

C

What is the time 5 hours 10 minutes after 9.05am? Look at this:

9.05am —5 hrs→ 2.05pm —10 mins→ 2.15pm

Do these in the same way.

1. 2 hours 15 minutes after 11.55am
2. 3 hours 45 minutes after 10.25am
3. 1 hour 40 minutes after 4.05am
4. 2 hours 20 minutes after 9.35am

D

1. The film started at 8.05pm. It lasted 2 hours 15 minutes. What time did it finish?
2. The cinema closes at 11.15pm and reopens at 2.00pm. How long is it closed?
3. The cleaners arrive 2 hours 30 minutes before the cinema reopens. What time do they arrive?

A

This graph shows how long some TV programmes last.

1. How many programmes are shown on the graph?
2. (a) Which is the longest programme?
   (b) How long does it last?
3. Does any programme last exactly 25 minutes?
4. How long does the Weather programme last?
5. Which programme lasts for a $\frac{1}{4}$ hour?
6. What do you notice about Play Bus and Mixing It?
7. How much longer than the News is The Aliens?

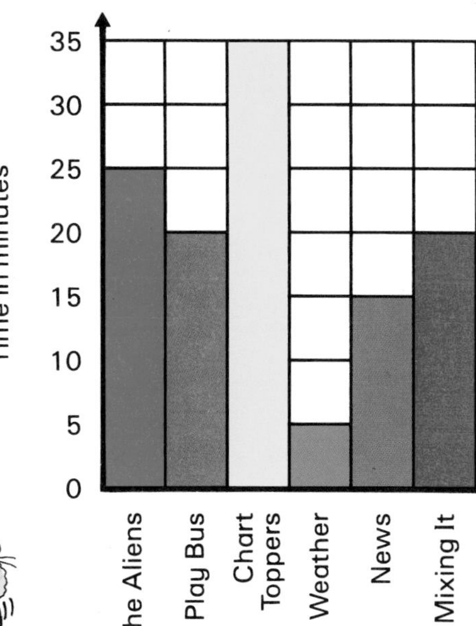

B

You will need some squared paper, coloured pencils and a timer. Now it's your turn to make a graph. Work with your group.

Each of you in turn must write down the name of your two favourite TV programmes. Take it in turns to time each other.

Draw axes like these and put in your information.

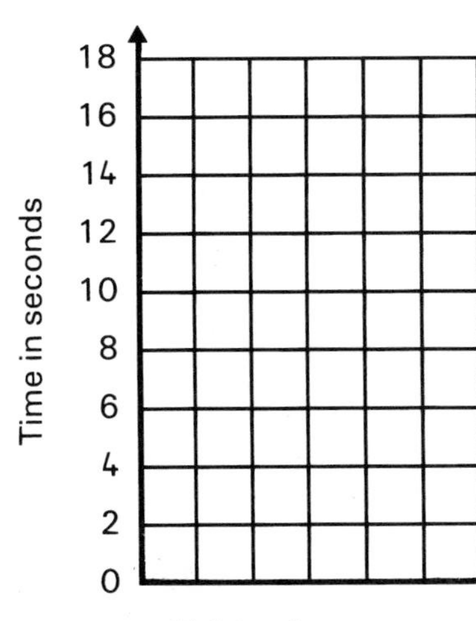

Now answer these questions:

1. Who was the slowest?
2. How can you tell this on the graph?
3. What does the shortest bar tell you?
4. Are any two bars the same height? If so, what does this tell you?

January						
S	M	T	W	Th	F	S
		1	2	3	4	5
6	7	8	9	10	11	12
13	14	15	16	17	18	19
20	21	22	23	24	25	26
27	28	29	30	31		

February						
S	M	T	W	Th	F	S
					1	2
3	4	5	6	7	8	9
10	11	12	13	14	15	16
17	18	19	20	21	22	23
24	25	26	27	28		

March						
S	M	T	W	Th	F	S
					1	2
3	4	5	6	7	8	9
10	11	12	13	14	15	16
17	18	19	20	21	22	23
24	25	26	27	28	29	30
31						

April						
S	M	T	W	Th	F	S
	1	2	3	4	5	6
7	8	9	10	11	12	13
14	15	16	17	18	19	20
21	22	23	24	25	26	27
28	29	30				

May						
S	M	T	W	Th	F	S
			1	2	3	4
5	6	7	8	9	10	11
12	13	14	15	16	17	18
19	20	21	22	23	24	25
26	27	28	29	30	31	

June						
S	M	T	W	Th	F	S
						1
2	3	4	5	6	7	8
9	10	11	12	13	14	15
16	17	18	19	20	21	22
23	24	25	26	27	28	29
30						

A

1. Copy and complete:

   (a) 17.3.91 *The 17th March was a Sunday.*
   (b) 12.6.91
   (c) 3.5.91
   (d) 18.2.91

2. Write the date one week and two weeks later than:

   (a) 4.1.91 (c) 13.3.91 (e) 16.5.91
   (b) 19.2.91 (d) 6.4.91 (f) 14.6.91

B

1. The twins went on holiday on 25.5.91 and returned on 8.6.91. How long were they away?
2. Josh was 10 on 2.3.91. Jenny was 10 on 30.3.91. How many weeks older than Jenny is Josh?
3. Danny went into hospital on 5.2.91 and came out on 19.3.91. How many weeks was he in hospital?
4. Grandad went to Australia on 11.5.91 and came back six weeks later. What date was that?
5. A fortnight is another way of writing two weeks.
   (a) We get a fortnight's holiday at Easter. It starts on March 27th. When do we go back?
   (b) The twins were catching a plane on 25.5.91. The tickets arrived a fortnight before. What date did the tickets arrive?

Comparing Fractions

You will need the worksheet called Fraction Wall.

A

Copy and complete these.
Use your worksheet to help you.

1. $1 = \frac{\square}{5}$
2. $1 = \frac{3}{\square}$
3. $1 = \frac{7}{\square}$
4. $1 = \frac{\square}{10}$
5. $1 = \frac{6}{\square}$
6. $1 = \frac{\square}{4}$
7. $1 = \frac{\square}{2}$
8. $1 = \frac{\square}{8}$
9. $1 = \frac{\square}{9}$
10. $1 = \frac{\square}{3}$

B

Copy and complete these using > or <.
Use your worksheet to help you.

1. $\frac{1}{8} \ (<) \ \frac{1}{2}$
2. $\frac{1}{4} \bigcirc \frac{1}{9}$
3. $\frac{1}{9} \bigcirc \frac{1}{10}$
4. $\frac{1}{5} \bigcirc \frac{1}{7}$
5. $\frac{1}{2} \bigcirc \frac{1}{4}$
6. $\frac{1}{6} \bigcirc \frac{1}{8}$
7. $\frac{1}{8} \bigcirc \frac{1}{10}$
8. $\frac{1}{3} \bigcirc \frac{1}{5}$
9. $\frac{1}{6} \bigcirc \frac{1}{4}$
10. $\frac{1}{4} \bigcirc \frac{2}{10}$
11. $\frac{3}{7} \bigcirc \frac{1}{5}$
12. $\frac{6}{10} \bigcirc \frac{7}{8}$
13. $\frac{2}{6} \bigcirc \frac{1}{4}$
14. $\frac{1}{2} \bigcirc \frac{6}{9}$
15. $\frac{2}{3} \bigcirc \frac{4}{7}$
16. $\frac{3}{5} \bigcirc \frac{3}{4}$
17. $\frac{3}{8} \bigcirc \frac{2}{7}$
18. $1 \bigcirc \frac{9}{10}$

Remember,
> means greater than
< means less than.

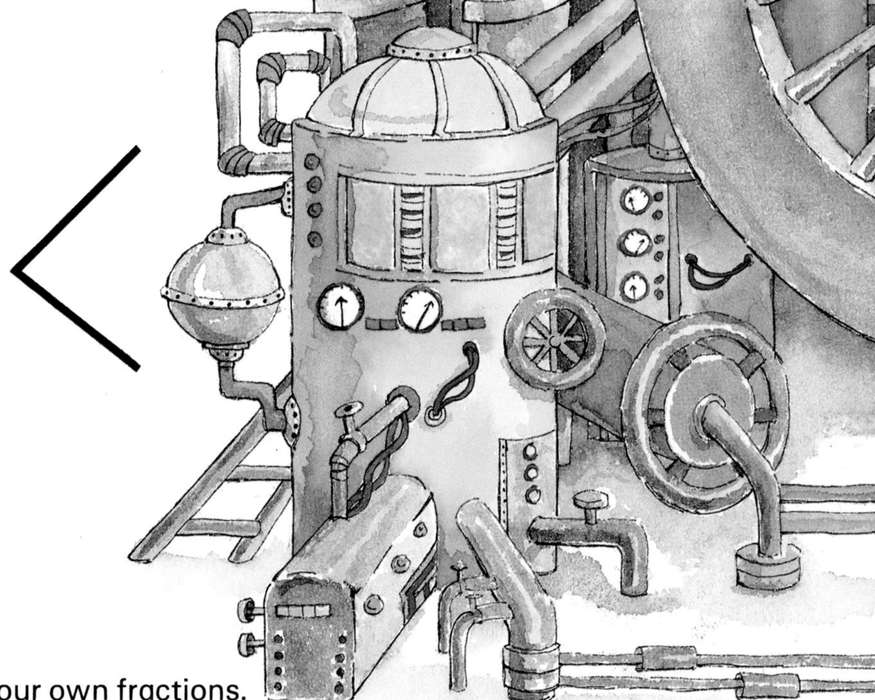

C

Copy and complete these by choosing your own fractions.
Use your worksheet to help you.

1. $\frac{1}{9} > \square$
2. $\frac{1}{8} < \square$
3. $\frac{1}{5} > \square$
4. $\frac{1}{6} > \square$
5. $\frac{1}{2} < \square$
6. $\frac{1}{3} < \square$
7. $\frac{3}{5} < \square$
8. $\frac{3}{8} > \square$
9. $\frac{1}{10} < \square$
10. $\frac{5}{10} < \square$
11. $\frac{2}{6} < \square$
12. $\frac{3}{4} > \square$
13. $\frac{2}{3} > \square$
14. $\frac{2}{7} < \square$
15. $\frac{4}{9} > \square$

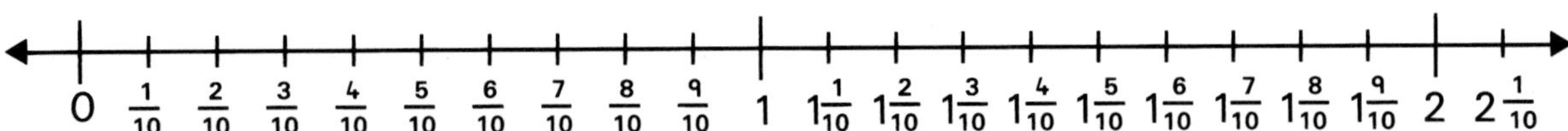

A

Write the answers to these. Use the number line to help you.

1. $\frac{5}{10} + \frac{2}{10}$
2. $\frac{3}{10} + \frac{4}{10}$
3. $\frac{7}{10} + \frac{1}{10}$
4. $\frac{9}{10} + \frac{1}{10}$
5. $\frac{6}{10} + \frac{3}{10}$
6. $\frac{8}{10} + \frac{4}{10}$
7. $\frac{6}{10} + \frac{8}{10}$
8. $\frac{5}{10} + \frac{7}{10}$
9. $\frac{9}{10} + \frac{9}{10}$
10. $\frac{8}{10} + \frac{5}{10}$

B

Now try these. Use the number line to help you.

1. $1\frac{9}{10} - \frac{6}{10}$
2. $\frac{5}{10} - \frac{4}{10}$
3. $\frac{8}{10} - \frac{5}{10}$
4. $\frac{7}{10} - \frac{2}{10}$
5. $\frac{6}{10} - \frac{6}{10}$
6. $1\frac{3}{10} - \frac{6}{10}$
7. $1\frac{4}{10} - \frac{3}{10}$
8. $1\frac{7}{10} - \frac{8}{10}$
9. $1\frac{2}{10} - \frac{5}{10}$
10. $2\frac{1}{10} - \frac{9}{10}$

C

Copy and complete.

1. $\frac{7}{10} + \frac{\square}{10} = 1$
2. $\frac{5}{10} + \frac{\square}{10} = 1$
3. $\frac{6}{10} + \frac{\square}{10} = 1$
4. $\frac{2}{10} + \frac{3}{10} + \frac{\square}{10} = 1$
5. $1\frac{4}{10} + \frac{\square}{10} = 2$
6. $1\frac{8}{10} + \frac{\square}{10} = 2$
7. Find 5 more ways of adding tenths to make 1.
8. Find 5 more ways of adding tenths to make 2.

Decimal Number Line

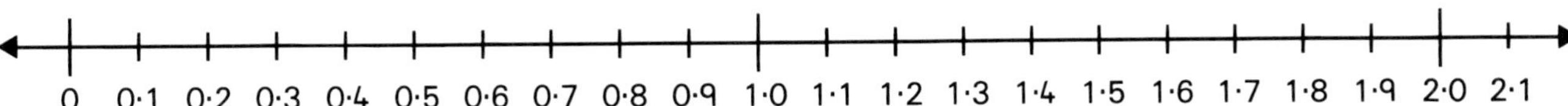

A

Copy and complete these using > or <.
Use the number line to help you.

1. 1·5 (<) 1·6
2. 1·1 ( ) 1·8
3. 1·3 ( ) 1·1
4. 0·6 ( ) 0·2
5. 1·0 ( ) 0·1
6. 0·9 ( ) 1·1
7. 0·2 ( ) 1·2
8. 0·2 ( ) 2·0

B

Copy and complete these by choosing your own decimals.
Use the number line to help you.

1. 1·9 > ☐
2. 0·5 < ☐
3. 1·0 > ☐
4. 0·7 < ☐
5. 1·6 < ☐
6. 0·2 > ☐

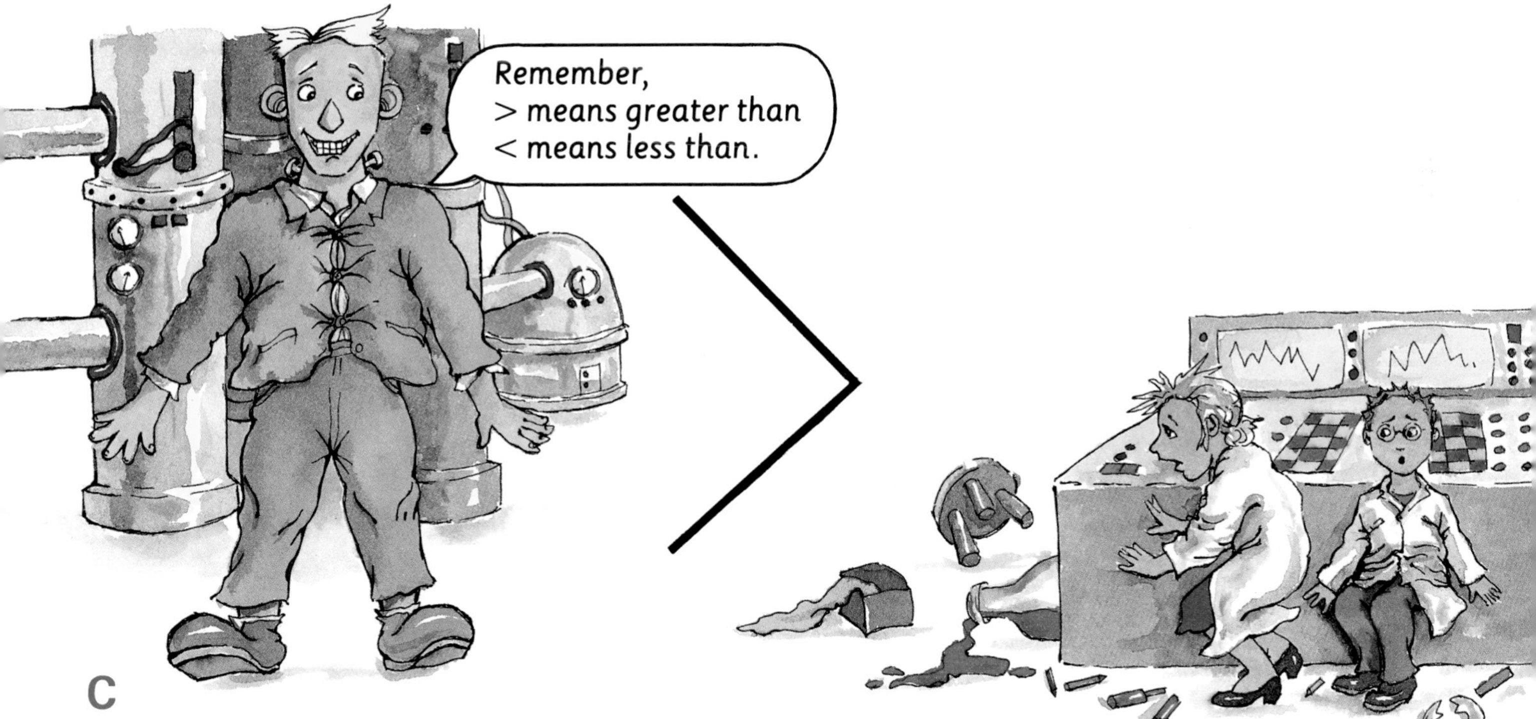

Remember,
> means greater than
< means less than.

C

Some of the numbers are missing on these decimal number lines.
Write down the number for each star.

1. 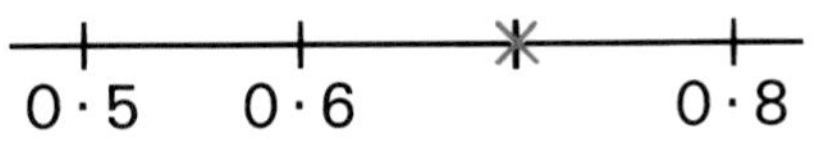 0·5, 0·6, ✳, 0·8
2. 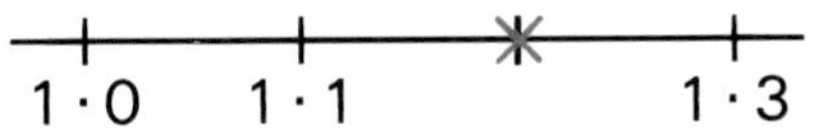 1·0, 1·1, ✳, 1·3
3. 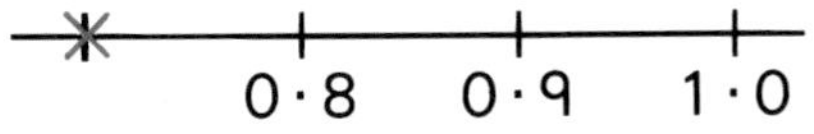 ✳, 0·8, 0·9, 1·0
4. 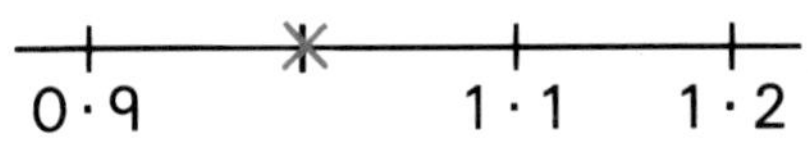 0·9, ✳, 1·1, 1·2
5. 2·2, ✳, 2·4, 2·5 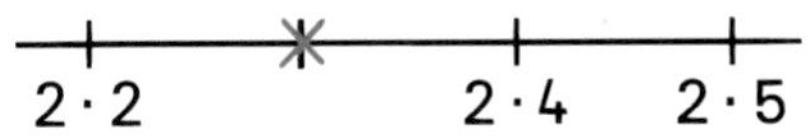
6. 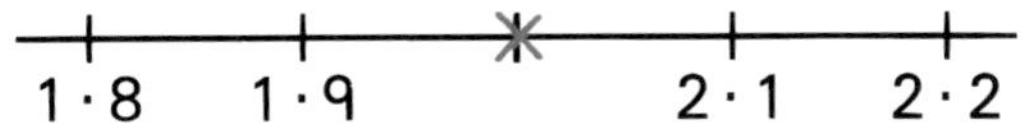 1·8, 1·9, ✳, 2·1, 2·2

A

Look at this cuboid.
It has been separated into slices.

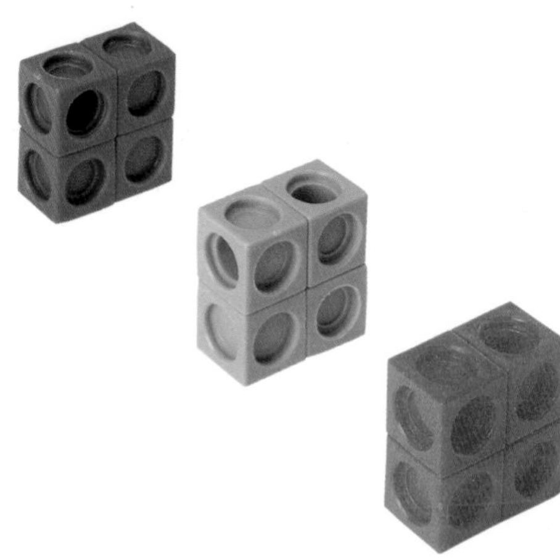

In each slice there are 2 rows of 2 cubes ⟶ (2 × 2) cubes ⟶ 4 cubes.

There are 3 slices ⟶ (3 × 4) cubes ⟶ 12 cubes.

So the volume of the cuboid is 12 cubes.

Copy and complete.

In each slice there are 2 rows of 3 cubes ⟶ (2 × 3) cubes ⟶ ____ cubes.

There are 5 slices ⟶ (5 × ____) cubes ⟶ ____ cubes.

Its volume is ____ cubes.

B

Now complete the same sentences for these cuboids.

1.

2.

3.

A

Find the volume of these cuboids.

Using the letters, write down the shapes in order of size. Start with the largest.

W

X

Y

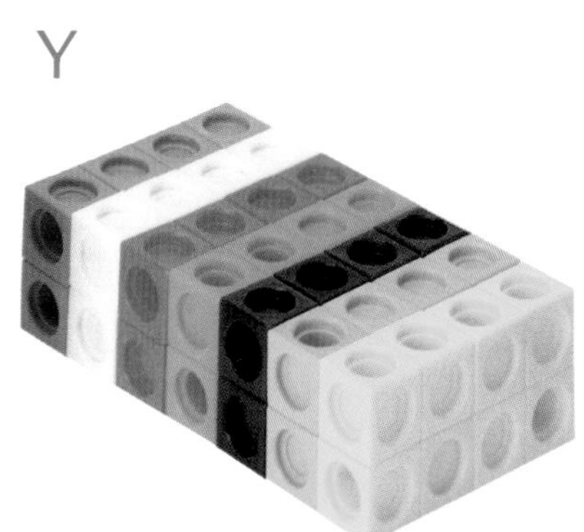

Z

B

1. Find the volume of these cubes. Copy and complete the table below.

A

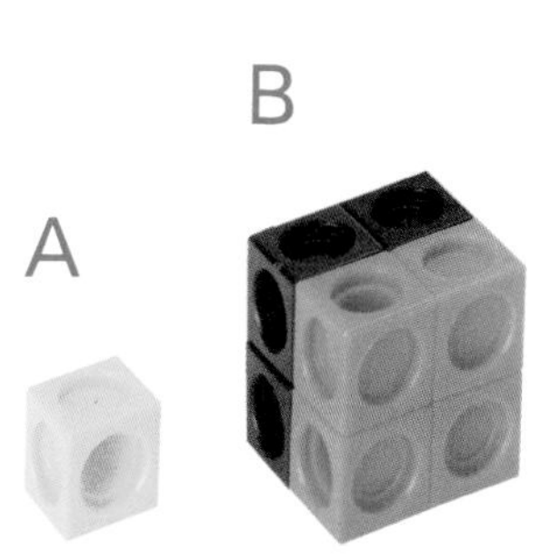

B

C

D

E

Cube	Length	Height	Width	Volume
A	*1 cube*	*1 cube*	*1 cube*	____ *cube*
B				
C				
D				
E				

2. Add five more rows to your table.

   Now find the volume of cubes F ⟶ J which have rows of 6 cubes, 7 cubes, 8 cubes, 9 cubes and 10 cubes.

   Write their details in the table.

   Can you see any patterns in your table?

A

Write down the area of each rectangle.

1\.

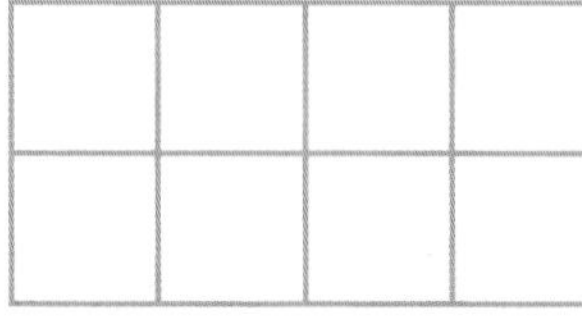

Area = 8 sq cm

2\.

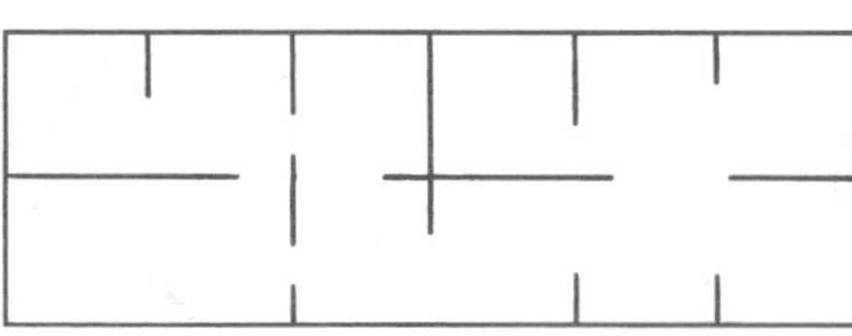

3\.

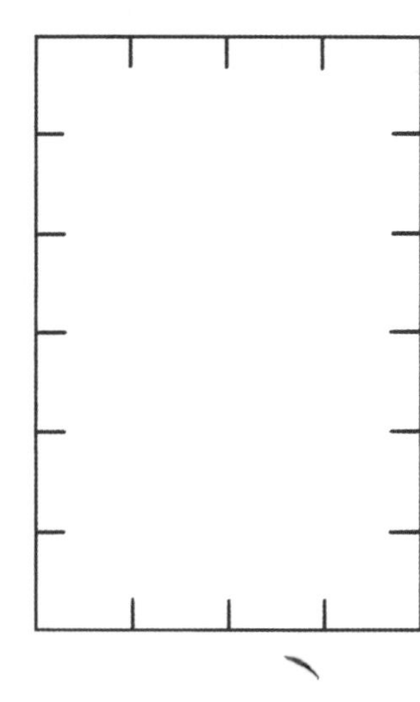

4\.

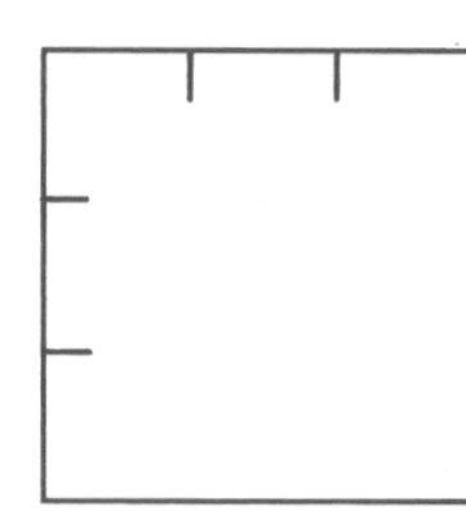

5\.

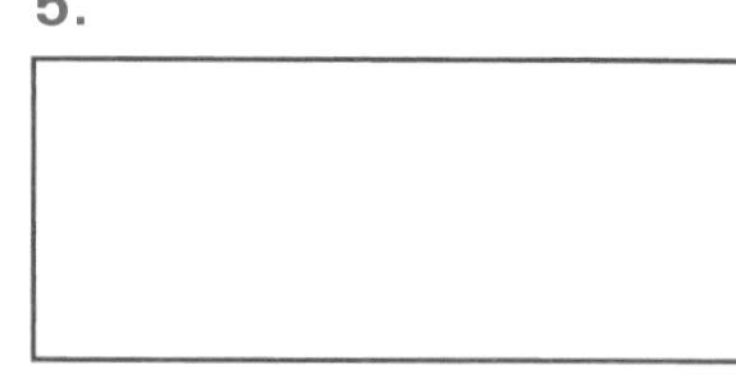

B

Now try these.

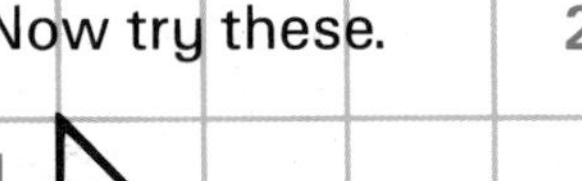

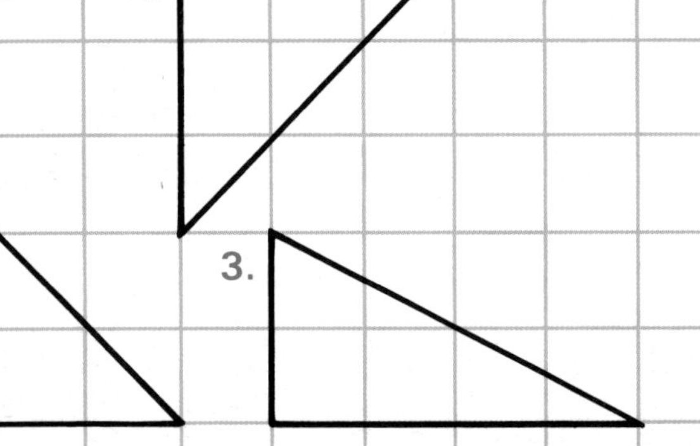

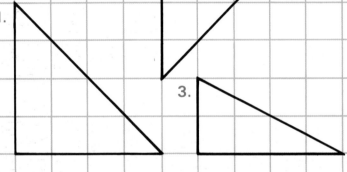

Remember, the triangles are half rectangles.

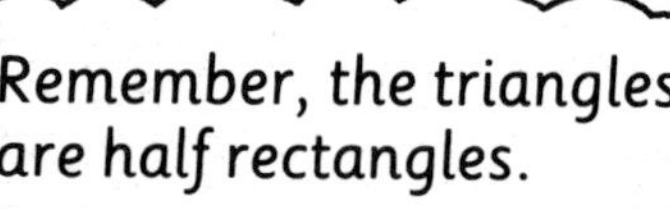

C

Look at this one.

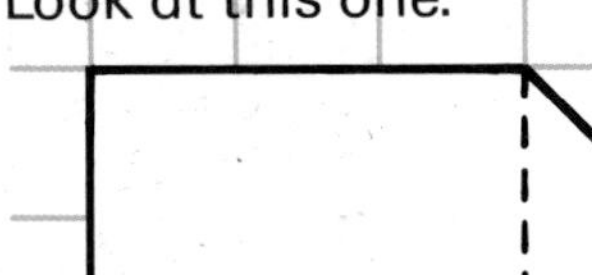

Area = area of rectangle + area of triangle
= 6 sq cm + 2 sq cm
= 8 sq cm

Do these in the same way.

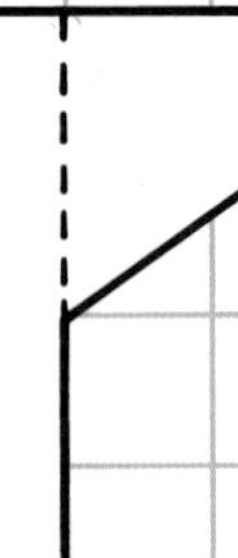

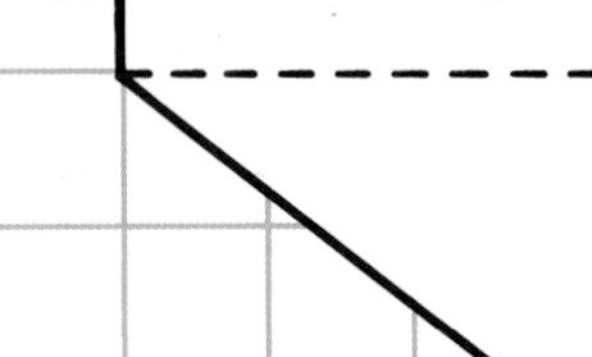

A

Complete the worksheet called Colour The Parallelograms before going on to Part B.

B

You will need scissors and glue.
Now we are going to find the areas of the parallelograms on your worksheet.

1. Cut out parallelogram A.

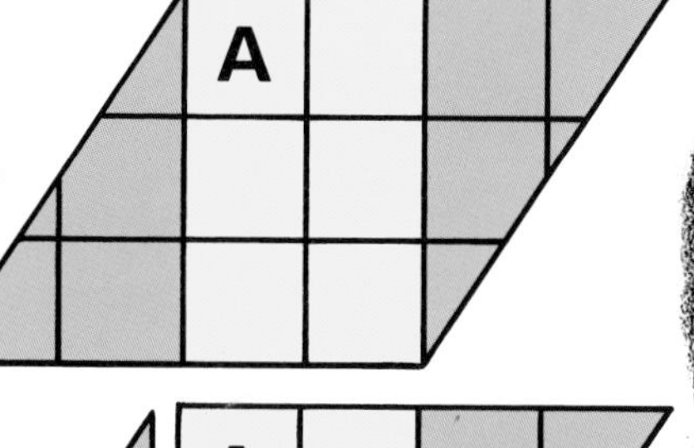

(a) Cut off one triangle.

(b) Move this triangle to the other side.

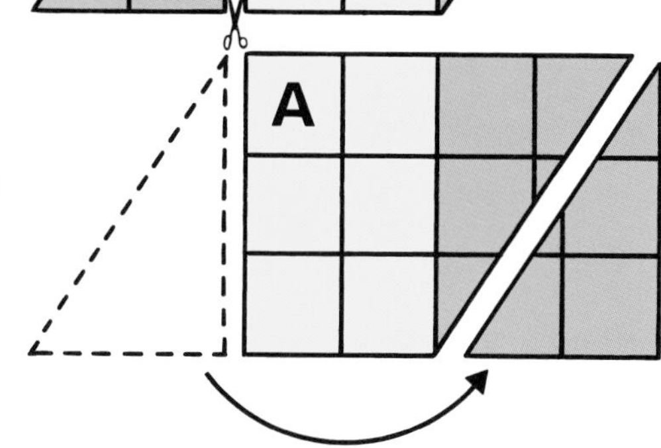

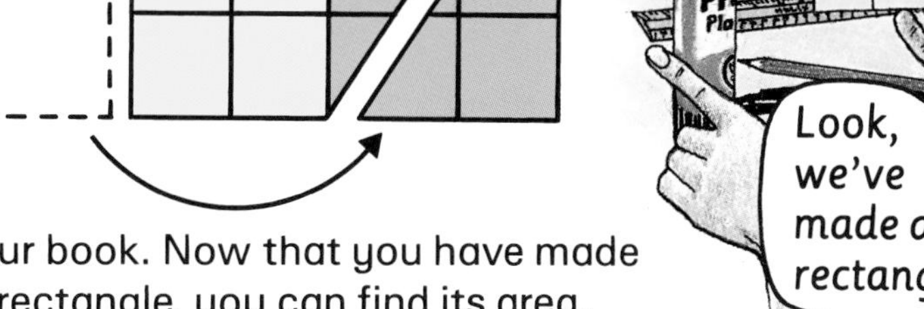

(c) Stick the rectangle in your book. Now that you have made the parallelogram into a rectangle, you can find its area.

(d) Write under your shape: *The area of parallelogram A is ______ sq cm.*

2. Now do the same for the other four parallelograms on your worksheet.

C

Can you work out the areas of these parallelograms?

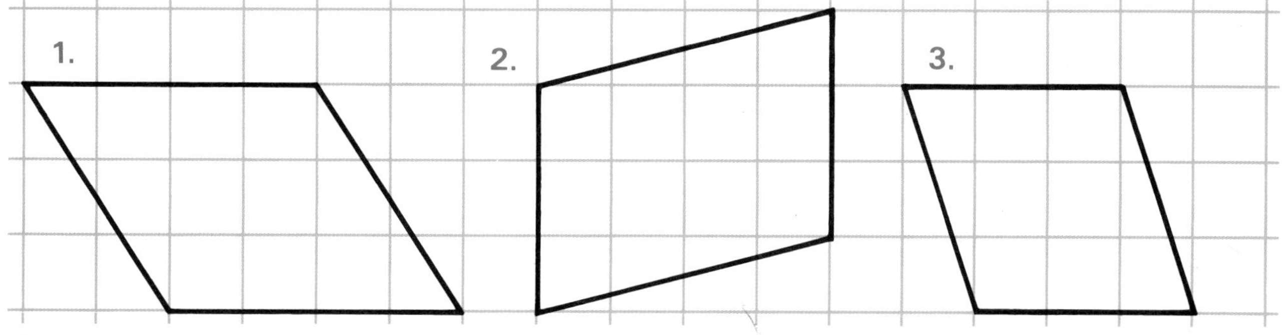

Angle Names

You will need a right angle tester.

A

Look at these three kinds of angle.

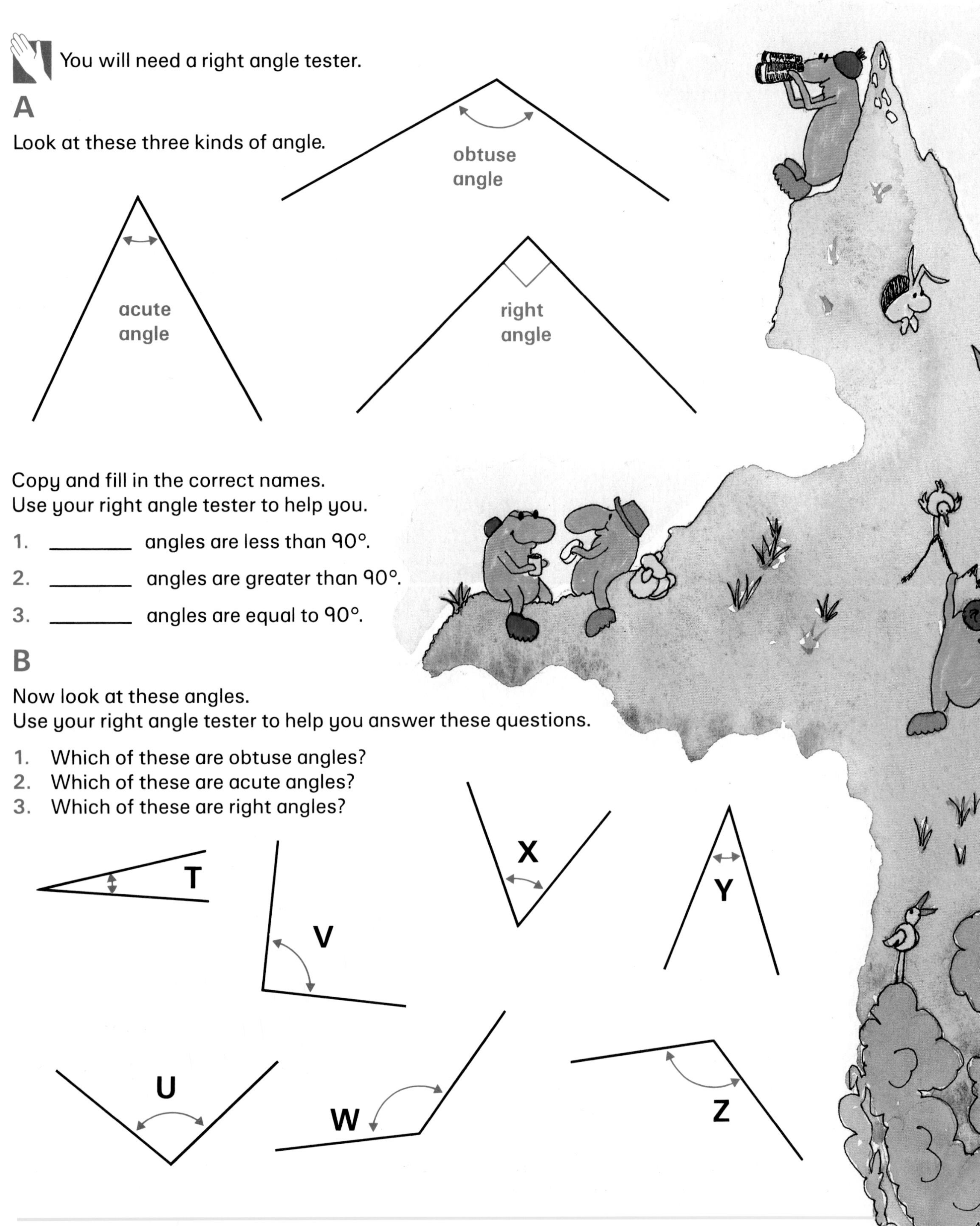

Copy and fill in the correct names.
Use your right angle tester to help you.

1. ________ angles are less than 90°.
2. ________ angles are greater than 90°.
3. ________ angles are equal to 90°.

B

Now look at these angles.
Use your right angle tester to help you answer these questions.

1. Which of these are obtuse angles?
2. Which of these are acute angles?
3. Which of these are right angles?

Mountain View

 You will need the worksheet called View Sheet and a paper fastener.

Cut out the pointers from the bottom of the worksheet.
Fix the two pointers to the centre (like the hands of a clock).

You are on the top of a mountain.
Answer the following questions using your worksheet.

A

You are facing North.
What angle do you turn through clockwise:

1. to face the bridge?
2. to face the lighthouse?
3. to face the school?
4. to face the railway station?
5. to face the pond?
6. to face West?

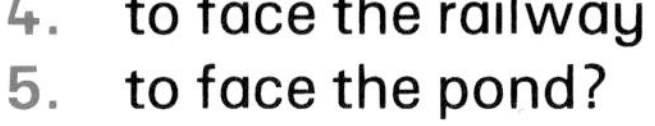

B

What angle do you turn through clockwise:

1. from the lighthouse to the railway station?
2. from the West to the pond?
3. from the village to the school?
4. from the pond to the church?
5. from the pond to the East?
6. from the wood to the bridge?

C

Face North again.

1. Turn clockwise through angles of 60°.
   Stop when you face North again.
   What do you face each time?
2. Turn clockwise through angles of 90°.
   Stop when you face North again.
   What do you face each time?
3. Turn clockwise through angles of 120°.
   Stop when you face North again.
   What do you face each time?
4. Now try turning clockwise through angles of 150°.
   Stop when you are facing North again.
   What do you face this time?
5. Move clockwise and face everything in turn on the worksheet.
   What angle do you move through each time?

Different Triangles

You will need a right angle tester and a ruler to help you answer these questions.

1. Which triangles are isosceles?
2. Which triangles are equilateral?
3. Which triangles have a right angle?
4. Which triangles have an obtuse angle?
5. Which triangles have only acute angles?

Remember, an isosceles triangle has two sides the same length, an equilateral triangle has three equal sides.

P

Q

U

T

R

W

V

S

X

Drawing Triangles

You will need some centimetre squared paper and a ruler.

A

Draw these triangles on squared paper.
The first picture shows you how to use the squares to help.

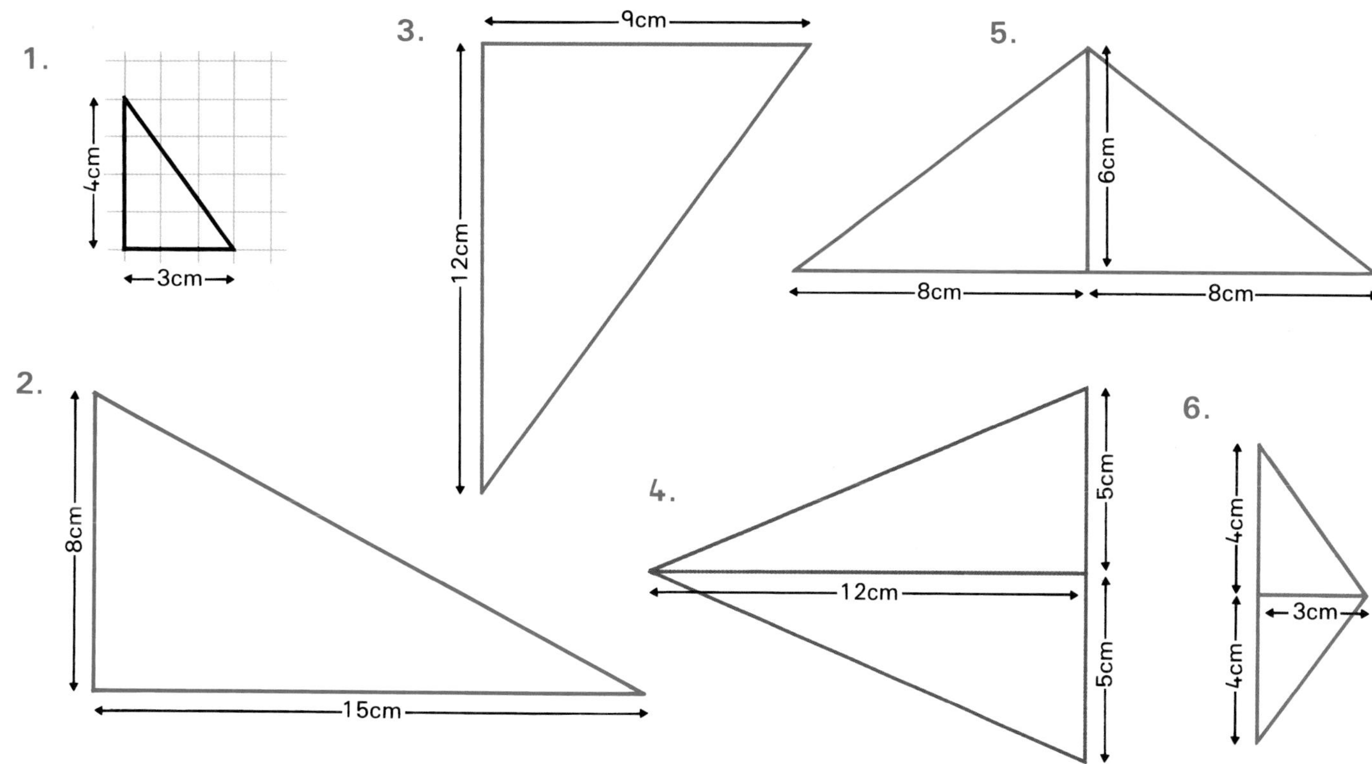

Measure the unmarked side or sides of each of your triangles.
Mark each length on your diagram.

B

Now draw these on squared paper.

1.
6cm
2cm
Start here.
4cm
4cm
3cm
6cm

2.
Start here.
5cm
4cm
5cm
5cm
2cm
10cm
4cm
6cm

Thousands Patterns

You will need your coloured-in Thousand Strips worksheet.

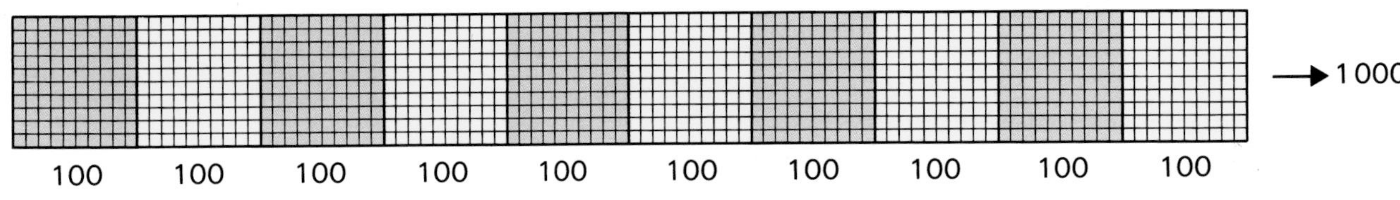

10 lots of 100 make 1000 so 10 × 100 = 1000

A

1. Copy and complete the table of hundreds

1 × 100 =
2 × 100 =
3 × 100 =
4 × 100 =
5 × 100 =
6 × 100 =
7 × 100 =
8 × 100 =
9 × 100 =
10 × 100 =

2. Now copy and complete the hundred times table

100 × 1 =
100 × 2 =
100 × 3 =
100 × 4 =
100 × 5 =
100 × 6 =
100 × 7 =
100 × 8 =
100 × 9 =
100 × 10 =

B

Use the worksheet called Machine Records to complete these tables.

In	Out
5	
	700
	300
9	
	1000
6	
	400
20	
	800

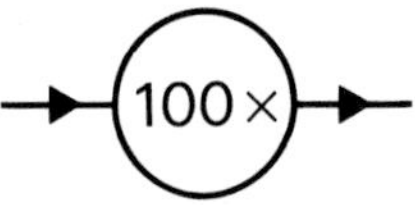

In	Out
7	
	500
10	
	600
4	
	2000
8	
	900
3	

C

Use your Thousand Strips worksheet to help you with these.

1. How many 50s in 2000?
2. How many 200s in 4000?
3. How many 20s in 1000?
4. How many 500s in 6000?
5. How many 250s in 3000?
6. ☐ × 100 = 2000
7. ☐ × 50 = 3000
8. ☐ × 500 = 7000
9. ☐ × 20 = 4000
10. ☐ × 250 = 5000

A

Look at these number lines. What does each letter represent?
Write the answer in your book like this: A = 3·5

1.
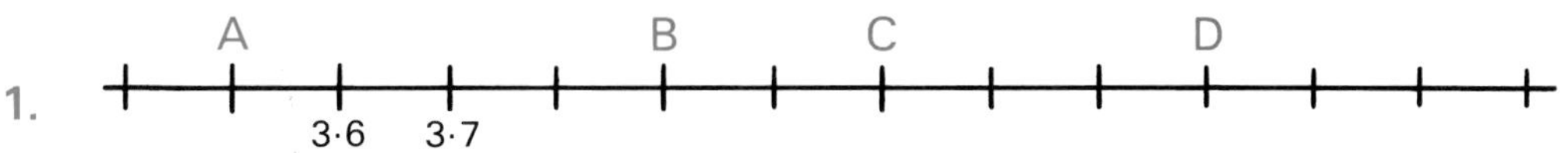

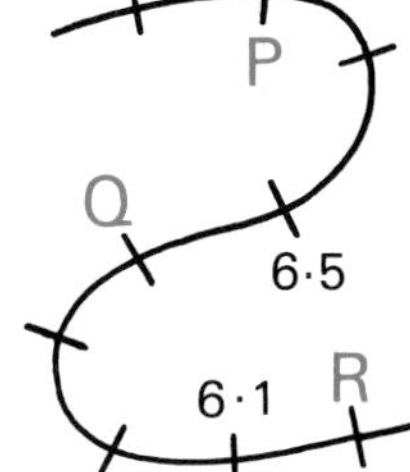

3. S T U

99·8 99·9

4.
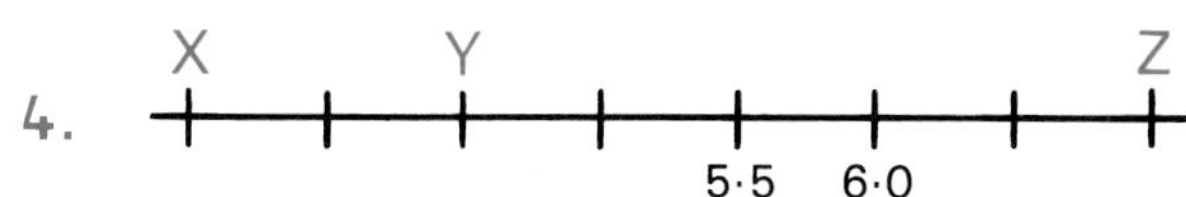

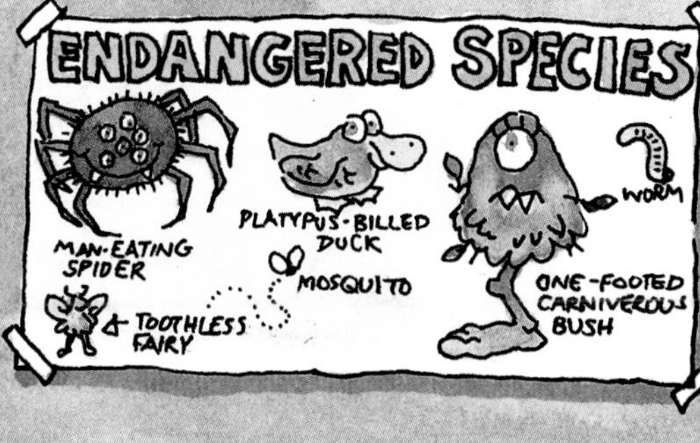

Some of these might have more than one answer.

B

Write down these numbers:

1. 1 unit smaller than 6·7
2. 1 tenth bigger than 3·4
3. 1 unit bigger than 9·2
4. 1 tenth smaller than 20·3
5. 3 tenths bigger than 11·8
6. A number between 8·4 and 9·5
7. A number between 17·3 and 18
8. A number between 9 and 10
9. A number between 18·5 and 18
10. A number between 28·1 and 27

C

Using the three digits 6, 9, and 2 each time, make a number that is:

1. near to 270
2. bigger than 950
3. close to 70
4. between 600 and 900
5. very close to 63
6. very close to 27
7. bigger than 92·6
8. between 29 and 30

A

You will need a counting board and some coloured cubes.

Use them to help you do these sums.

1. 6535 + 2842 = ______
2. 2824 + 5673 = ______
3. 3905 + 4892 = ______
4. 6664 + 2713 = ______
5. 4548 + 2725 = ______
6. 6863 + 2376 = ______
7. 4787 + 2758 = ______
8. 4733 + 3888 = ______
9. 2788 + 4286 = ______
10. 3618 + 2983 = ______

B

Which pairs of numbers from the first computer screen when added together, give the numbers on the second?

C

Copy these and fill in the missing numbers.

1.
```
   3 7 3 5
 + □ 2 □ 3
   9 □ 7 □
```

2.
```
   5 6 8 6
 + □ 2 □ 9
   8 □ 4 □
     1 1
```

3.
```
   □ □ □ □
 + 4 1 3 4
   7 8 0 9
   1
```

4.
```
   5 □ 6 □
 + □ 2 □ 8
   8 4 9 2
     1
```

5.
```
   □ 7 6 4
 + 2 □ □ □
   6 0 8 7
   1
```

6.
```
   □ 6 9 □
 + 2 □ 0 8
   8 0 □ 3
   1 1 1
```

 You will need the worksheet called Machine Records.

A

Here is Toni's +1234 machine.

Fill in a table for it.

In	Out
3742	
5963	
2479	
4892	
8003	
999	

B

Toni tried to put the output numbers straight back into the machine.
She put in 2653 and out came 3887.
Then she put 3887 back into the machine and so on.
The machine always stops working when it reaches 10000.

1. Fill in a table to show all the numbers it printed out.
2. Now fill in a table to show what happens if Toni puts 1361 into the machine.

In	Out
2653	3887
3887	

C

 You will need a calculator.

Can you do these in your head? Just write the answers.

1. 3629 + 2000
2. 3000 + 1999
3. 5142 + 111
4. 3333 + 3333
5. 2943 + 3001
6. 2361 + 40
7. Now check your answers with a calculator.
8. Choose one of the sums and write a real-life story about it.

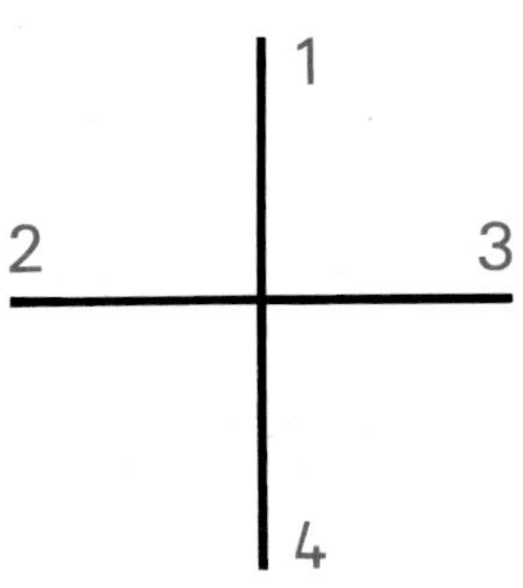

Here are the numbers 1, 2, 3, 4 arranged on a cross so that each line adds up to 5.

$$1 + 4 = 5$$
$$2 + 3 = 5$$

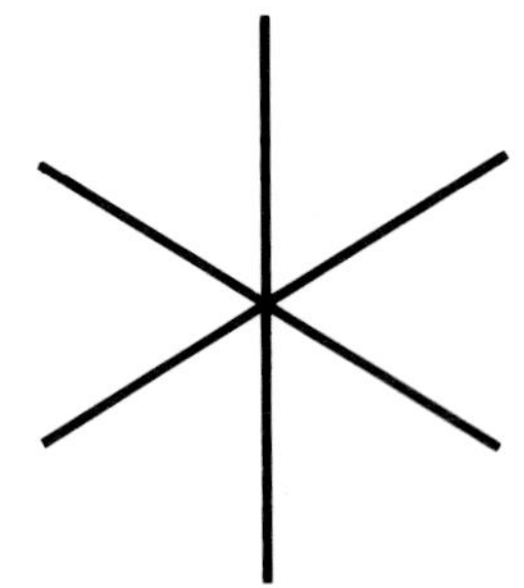

1. Copy this star.
   Use the numbers 1, 2, 3, 4, 5, 6.
   Arrange them so that each line adds up to 7.

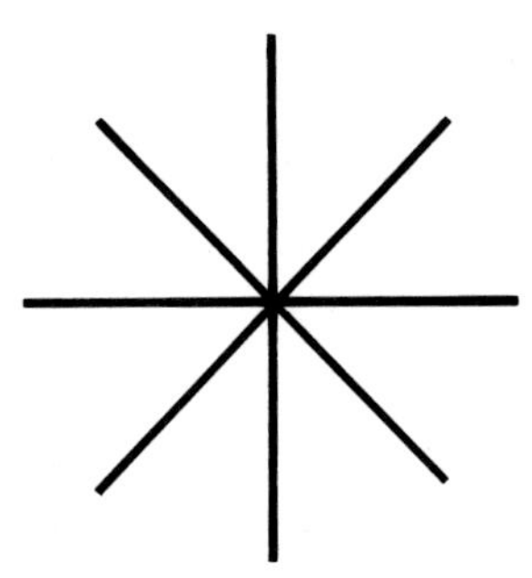

2. Copy this star.
   Use the numbers 1, 2, 3, 4, 5, 6, 7, 8.
   Arrange them so that each line adds up to the same number.

3. Draw a star to use with the numbers 1, 2, 3, 4, 5, 6, 7, 8, 9, 10.
   Arrange them so that each line adds up to the same number.

4. Draw a table like this and fill in your results.

Highest number on star	Lines add up to
4	5
6	
8	
10	

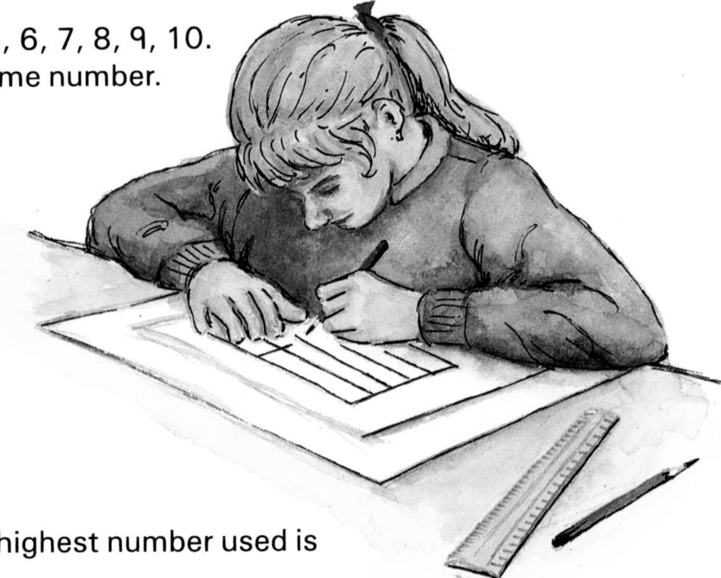

5. What do you think the lines will add up to if the highest number used is

   (a) 16? (b) 28?

6. Draw an 8 line star to check your answer to 5(a).

A

Try these.

1. 5295 − 1870 = ____
2. 7649 − 3927 = ____
3. 6757 − 1834 = ____
4. 5087 − 1848 = ____
5. 8302 − 6913 = ____
6. 9415 − 5867 = ____
7. 6217 − 3001 = ____
8. 6854 − 5867 = ____
9. 1870 − 1619 = ____
10. 7130 − 3793 = ____

B

Here are 4 subtractions and their answers, but they are mixed up.
Copy them into your book.
Draw a straight line from each question to its correct answer.

Questions	Answers
8025 − 3218	4158
8941 − 2873	6068
9162 − 3392	4807
7130 − 2972	5770

C

Work out the answers to these.

1. Mount Everest is 8848m high. Ben Nevis is 1343m high.
   How much further would you have to climb to get to the top of Mount Everest?
2. Rome is 1809km away from London. Paris is 449km away from London.
   How much further away from London is Rome than Paris?
3. At its greatest depth, the Atlantic Ocean is 8381m deep, and the Arctic Ocean is 5450m deep.
   If a ship sank at both of these places, how much further would it have to sink to get to the bottom of the Atlantic Ocean?
4. Guy Fawkes was born in 1570. How long ago was this?
5. There are 9806 students at Cambridge University and 7188 students at Bristol University.
   How many fewer students are there at Bristol University?

Approximations

A

We do not always have to be accurate.
Sometimes we can approximate.

Let's find an approximation for this sum:
82 − 58

> Write each number to the nearest ten.
> 82 → 80 58 → 60
> Then subtract the new numbers.
> 80 − 60 = 20

So 82 − 58 is approximately 20.

Now find approximations for these:

1. 81 − 67
2. 94 − 28
3. 77 − 38
4. 63 − 29
5. 42 − 16
6. 93 − 37
7. 83 − 32
8. 95 − 41
9. 92 − 55
10. 77 − 13
11. 63 − 25
12. 76 − 44

B

Let's find an approximation for this sum:
583 − 297

> Write each number to the nearest hundred.
> 583 → 600 297 → 300
> Then subtract the new numbers.
> 600 − 300 = 300

So 583 − 297 is approximately 300.

Now find approximations for these:

1. 577 − 218
2. 497 − 208
3. 917 − 384
4. 777 − 329
5. 720 − 199
6. 580 − 283
7. 493 − 95
8. 713 − 476
9. 527 − 264
10. 947 − 235
11. 975 − 616
12. 821 − 467

C

 You will need a calculator.

Find accurate answers to all the sums in Parts A and B.
Write the approximation next to the accurate answer for each sum.
How near are the approximations?

A

Do you remember these?

$$\begin{array}{r} 386 \\ \times \quad 4 \\ \hline 1544 \\ \hline {\scriptstyle 3\,2} \end{array} \qquad \begin{array}{r} 576 \\ \times \quad 8 \\ \hline 4608 \\ \hline {\scriptstyle 6\,4} \end{array}$$

In these sums the thousands build up.

Copy and complete these in the same way.

1. 2 × 552
2. 5 × 236
3. 3 × 647
4. 4 × 543
5. 8 × 159
6. 9 × 237
7. 7 × 315
8. 6 × 392
9. 8 × 732
10. 7 × 844
11. 9 × 803
12. 8 × 971

B

Copy these and fill in the missing numbers.

1. $\begin{array}{r} 3\,3\,\square \\ \times \quad 6 \\ \hline 2\,\square\,0\,4 \\ \hline {\scriptstyle 2\,2} \end{array}$

2. $\begin{array}{r} 4\,\square\,7 \\ \times \quad 8 \\ \hline 3\,5\,7\,\square \\ \hline {\scriptstyle 3\,5} \end{array}$

3. $\begin{array}{r} 9\,2\,\square \\ \times \quad 5 \\ \hline 4\,6\,\square\,0 \\ \hline {\scriptstyle 1\,3} \end{array}$

4. $\begin{array}{r} \square\,7\,5 \\ \times \quad 7 \\ \hline 3\,3\,\square\,5 \\ \hline {\scriptstyle 5\,3} \end{array}$

C

1. There are 459 cars parked in the leisure centre car park on Monday. There are 4 wheels on each car. How many wheels are there altogether?
2. On Tuesday 492 cars are parked in the car park. Each car has two headlamps. How many headlamps are there altogether?
3. On Monday each car had 4 passengers. On Tuesday each car had 5 passengers. How many passengers were there altogether on Monday and Tuesday?
4. The leisure centre is open for 301 days a year except for leap years when it is open for one more day. How many days is it open for in 4 years? (One of those years is a leap year.)
5. Make up a problem about the leisure centre for 7 × 246. Work out the answer.

A

Try these by splitting sets.
Do each one in two different ways.

1. 12 × 5
2. 15 × 4
3. 14 × 6
4. 17 × 8
5. 16 × 3
6. 15 × 9
7. 19 × 7
8. 18 × 8
9. 17 × 6
10. 16 × 8

Which is the easiest way to split?

B

The table of tens is an easy one.
So splits which have 10 × in them are easy.

Copy and complete these.
Use a split with 10 each time.
The first two are started for you.

1. 13 × 6 → 3 sets of 6 → ☐
   → 10 sets of 6 → ☐
   Total ___

2. 14 × 8 → 4 sets of 8 → ☐
   → 10 sets of 8 → ☐
   Total ___

3. 15 × 8
4. 12 × 9
5. 13 × 8
6. 14 × 7
7. 17 × 5
8. 11 × 9
9. 13 × 7
10. 12 × 8

At The Leisure Centre

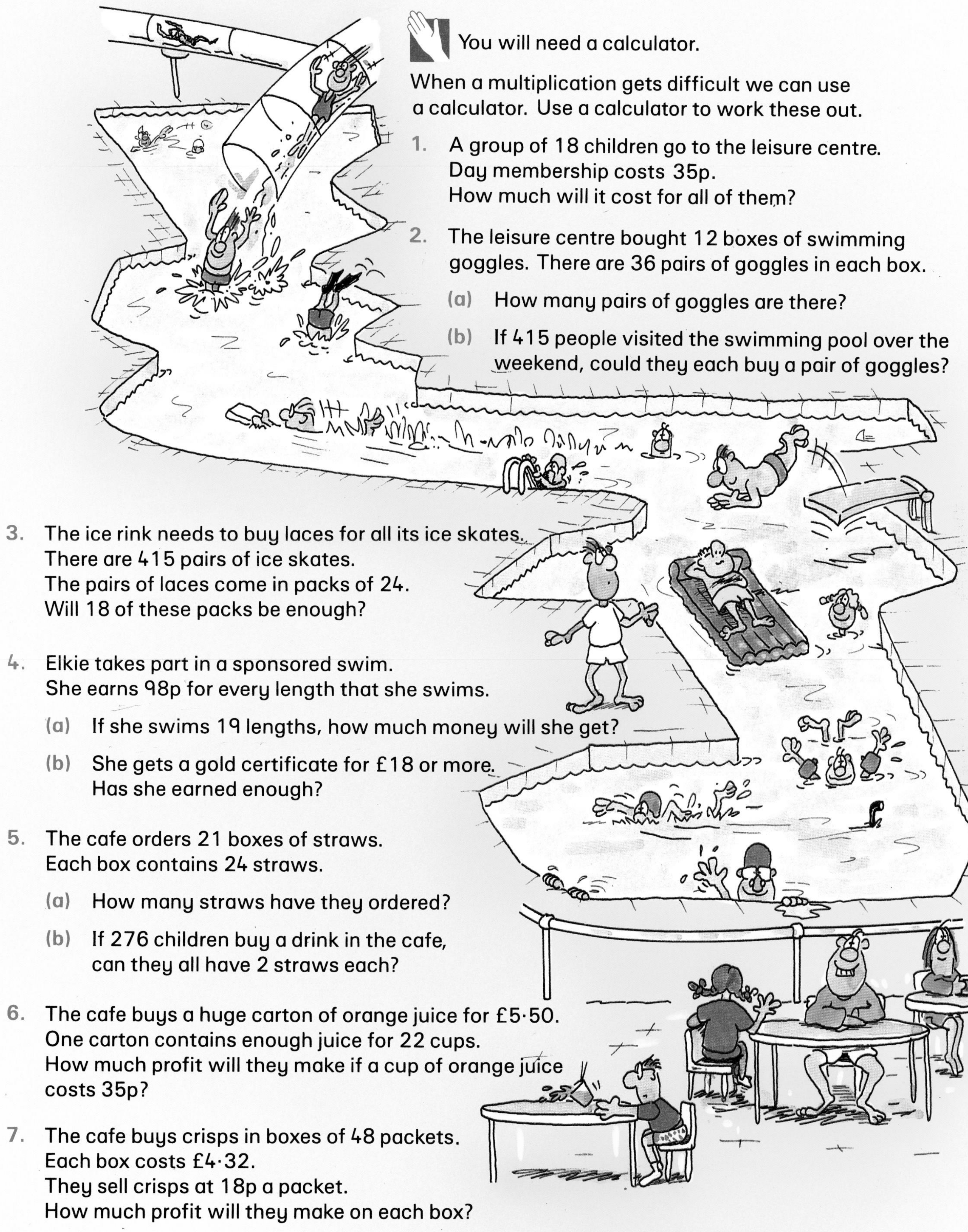

You will need a calculator.

When a multiplication gets difficult we can use a calculator. Use a calculator to work these out.

1. A group of 18 children go to the leisure centre. Day membership costs 35p. How much will it cost for all of them?

2. The leisure centre bought 12 boxes of swimming goggles. There are 36 pairs of goggles in each box.
   (a) How many pairs of goggles are there?
   (b) If 415 people visited the swimming pool over the weekend, could they each buy a pair of goggles?

3. The ice rink needs to buy laces for all its ice skates. There are 415 pairs of ice skates. The pairs of laces come in packs of 24. Will 18 of these packs be enough?

4. Elkie takes part in a sponsored swim. She earns 98p for every length that she swims.
   (a) If she swims 19 lengths, how much money will she get?
   (b) She gets a gold certificate for £18 or more. Has she earned enough?

5. The cafe orders 21 boxes of straws. Each box contains 24 straws.
   (a) How many straws have they ordered?
   (b) If 276 children buy a drink in the cafe, can they all have 2 straws each?

6. The cafe buys a huge carton of orange juice for £5·50. One carton contains enough juice for 22 cups. How much profit will they make if a cup of orange juice costs 35p?

7. The cafe buys crisps in boxes of 48 packets. Each box costs £4·32. They sell crisps at 18p a packet. How much profit will they make on each box?

Here are some division stories.
Write the number which goes in each box. Think carefully!

1. Torch batteries come in packs of 6. We must buy ☐ packs to get 57 batteries.

2. Plastic forks come in packs of 10. We must buy ☐ packs to get 59 forks.

3. 51 pies put onto trays of 8 is ☐ full trays and ☐ pies left over.

4. There are 35 children. We need ☐ tents if we put 4 children in each tent.

5. 43 burgers shared equally between 6 children is ☐ each.

6. 69 bottles of pop put into crates of 7 bottles is ☐ full crates and ☐ bottles left over.

7. 46 jacket potatoes shared equally between 5 children is ☐ each.

8. We cannot share 36 sleeping bags equally between ☐ tents.

9. We cannot share 60 tent pegs equally between ☐ tents.

10. 30 girls can make ☐ groups of 4.

You will need a calculator.

A

Look at this division: 57 ÷ 4
We can split 57 to make the division easier, like this:

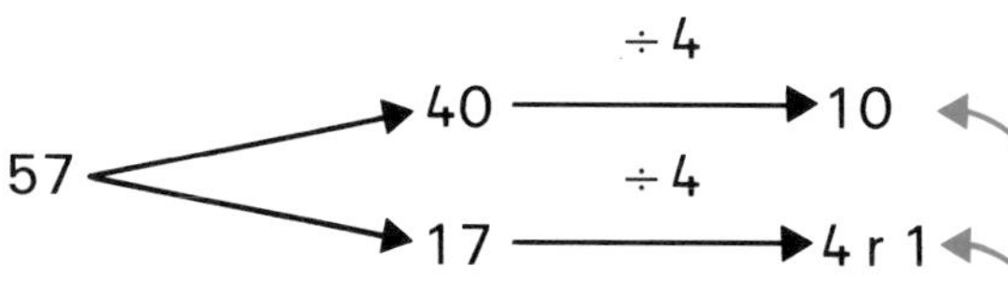

Now we add these answers together.

So 57 ÷ 4 = 14 r 1

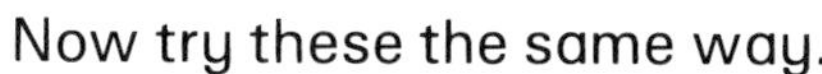

Now try these the same way.
Use your calculator to check your answers, but watch out if there are remainders.

1. 67 ÷ 4
2. 89 ÷ 6
3. 94 ÷ 7
4. 90 ÷ 8
5. 96 ÷ 9
6. 73 ÷ 5
7. 96 ÷ 6
8. 65 ÷ 5
9. 86 ÷ 7
10. 96 ÷ 8
11. 89 ÷ 7
12. 91 ÷ 8

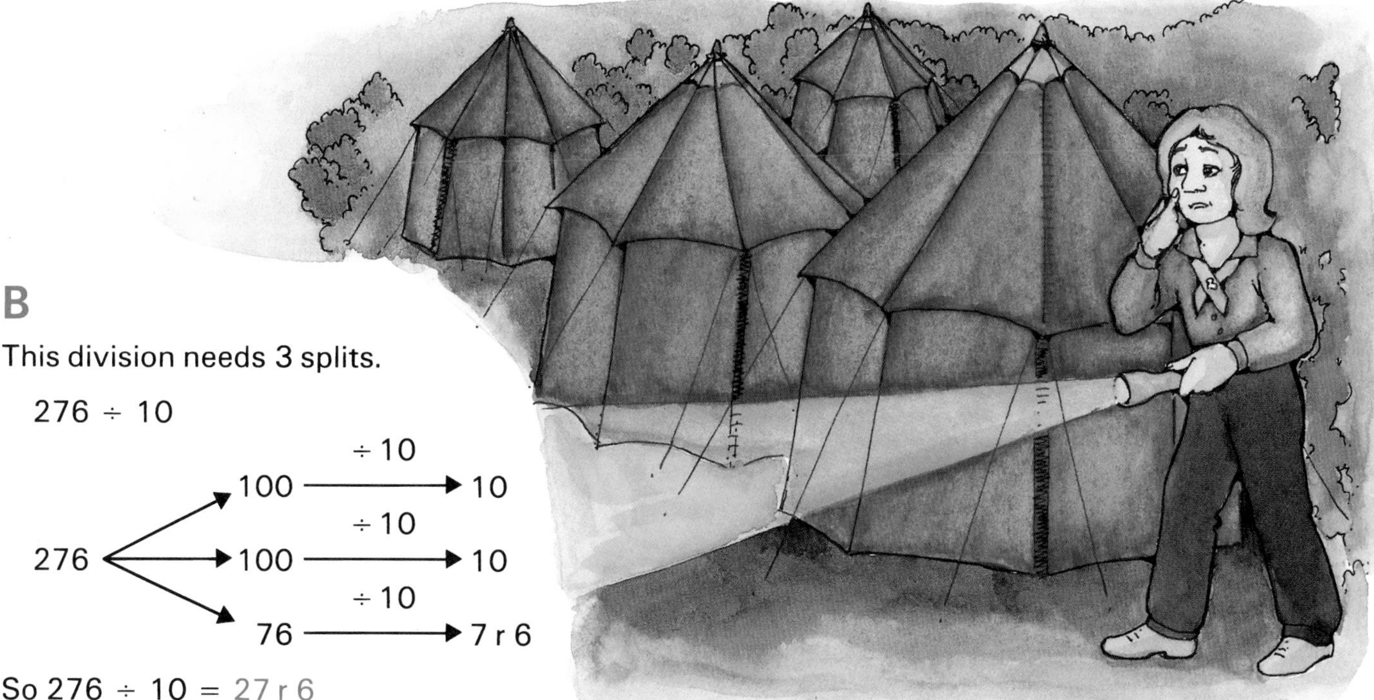

B

This division needs 3 splits.

276 ÷ 10

276 → 100 —÷10→ 10
276 → 100 —÷10→ 10
276 → 76 —÷10→ 7 r 6

So 276 ÷ 10 = 27 r 6

Now try these. Use your calculator again to check your answers.
Some may need more than 3 splits!

1. 147 ÷ 10
2. 173 ÷ 10
3. 189 ÷ 10
4. 216 ÷ 10
5. 359 ÷ 10
6. 307 ÷ 10
7. 512 ÷ 10
8. 423 ÷ 10
9. 399 ÷ 10
10. 471 ÷ 10
11. 382 ÷ 10
12. 499 ÷ 10

You will need the worksheet called Machine Records.

A

Here is a ÷10 machine.

1. Fill in a table for the machine.

In	Out
50	
80	
70	
30	
90	
40	
20	

Now we link it to a 10× machine.

2. Fill in a table for the double machine.

In	Middle	Out
4	40	4
7		
5		
8		
2		
9		
6		
10		

Can you see that this is a lazy machine?

B

If we put bigger numbers into the double machine in Part A, the Out numbers will still be the same as the In numbers we put in — because it is lazy.

1. Fill in a table for the double machine.

In	Middle	Out
12		12
18		18
27		27
31		31
56		56
65		65
74		74

2. Use the table to answer these divisions.

(a) 650 ÷ 10
(b) 310 ÷ 10
(c) 180 ÷ 10
(d) 740 ÷ 10
(e) 270 ÷ 10
(f) 560 ÷ 10

Can you see a pattern? Talk to your teacher about it.

3. Use the pattern to answer these.

(a) 890 ÷ 10
(b) 320 ÷ 10
(c) 480 ÷ 10
(d) 990 ÷ 10
(e) 260 ÷ 10
(f) 870 ÷ 10

A

 You will need the worksheet called Decimal Counting Boards.

Richard was doing some divisions. This is how he used a counting board to show what he did.

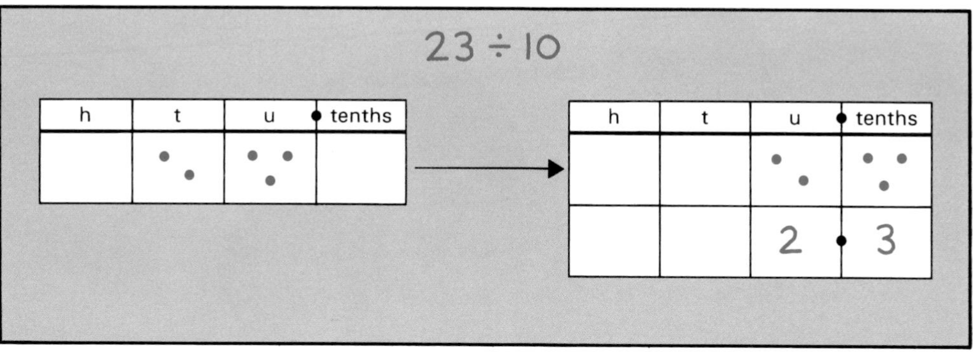

Use the counting boards to help you do these.

1. 29 ÷ 10
2. 87 ÷ 10
3. 96 ÷ 10
4. 44 ÷ 10
5. 64 ÷ 10
6. 39 ÷ 10
7. 72 ÷ 10
8. 13 ÷ 10
9. 8 ÷ 10
10. 6 ÷ 10
11. 354 ÷ 10
12. 786 ÷ 10
13. 573 ÷ 10
14. 607 ÷ 10
15. 934 ÷ 10
16. 214 ÷ 10
17. 438 ÷ 10
18. 822 ÷ 10
19. 745 ÷ 10
20. 303 ÷ 10

B

Look at your answers for Part B on Page 55: Splitting And Dividing.
Now write the answers again in decimals by dividing the remainders.

C

You will need the worksheet called Machine Records.

Fill in tables for these machines.

1.

In	Out
64	6·4
108	
326	
890	
507	

2.

In	Out
	7·6
	50·2
	78·9
	75
	30·1

Calculator Division

A

Work these out on your calculator.

1. 4536 ÷ 7
2. 4279 ÷ 11
3. 16188 ÷ 19
4. 23064 ÷ 24
5. 25704 ÷ 34
6. 50594 ÷ 41

B

Now try these on your calculator. These answers should all be short decimals.

1. 952 ÷ 20
2. 1737 ÷ 18
3. 956 ÷ 16
4. 7304 ÷ 16
5. 865 ÷ 20
6. 7392 ÷ 15
7. 9173 ÷ 4
8. 4584 ÷ 25

C

Work these out on the calculator. This time you will get long decimals.
Only write down the first two numbers after the decimal point.

1. 562 ÷ 23
2. 877 ÷ 28
3. 1235 ÷ 47
4. 5689 ÷ 39
5. 8521 ÷ 41
6. 6532 ÷ 29
7. 7852 ÷ 31
8. 9571 ÷ 43

D

Sometimes the long decimals have patterns in them! Work out each of these.
Write down what the pattern is.

1. 19 ÷ 9
2. 58 ÷ 18
3. 196 ÷ 36
4. 240 ÷ 45
5. 7903 ÷ 63
6. 2817 ÷ 27

These decimals have some harder patterns. Write about them too.

7. 95 ÷ 11
8. 122 ÷ 22
9. 565 ÷ 55
10. 3941 ÷ 77
11. 8952 ÷ 99
12. 7812 ÷ 33

Look really carefully here. Can you see the pattern each time?

13. 524 ÷ 37
14. 986 ÷ 74
15. 9550 ÷ 111
16. 2153 ÷ 37
17. 3712 ÷ 111
18. 5642 ÷ 74

A Lot Of Multiplication

A

1. Work out 7 × 41 without using your calculator.
2. Now press these buttons: 7 [×] 41 [=]
   Did the calculator get the same answer as you?
3. Now try 41 × 7 on the calculator. What do you notice?
4. Work out each of these:

(a)	6 × 53	(d)	82 × 9	(g)	7 × 59	(j)	67 × 9
(b)	53 × 6	(e)	8 × 75	(h)	59 × 7	(k)	47 × 8
(c)	9 × 82	(f)	75 × 8	(i)	9 × 67	(l)	8 × 47

5. What do you notice about the answers?
   Write about it in your book.

B

Here is a 10× machine: In → (10×) → Out

We can link three of them together:

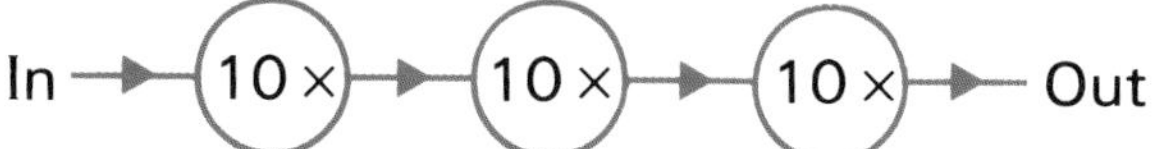

1. Copy and complete this table for the linked machines, using your calculator.

In			Out
42	420	4200	42000
29			
58			
87			
273			
681			
575			
714			

2. Write about the pattern.

C

1. Apples come in boxes of 36.
   Use your calculator to work out this ready reckoner.

   1 box holds 36 apples
   2 boxes hold ____ apples
   3 boxes hold ____ apples

   Go on until you reach the line: 20 boxes hold ____ apples.

2. Now answer these:

   (a) How many boxes must be bought to get 300 apples?
   (b) How many boxes must be bought to get 700 apples?

A

You will need the worksheet called Machine Records and some squared paper.

1. Here is a 30× machine.

Fill in this table for the 30× machine, using your calculator.

In	Out
29	
38	
47	
56	
65	
74	

2. Now look at this double machine.

(a) Fill in a table for this double machine. Put in the same numbers as in question 1.

(b) What happens? Can you explain why?

3. Now do the same for:

4. Look at this double machine.

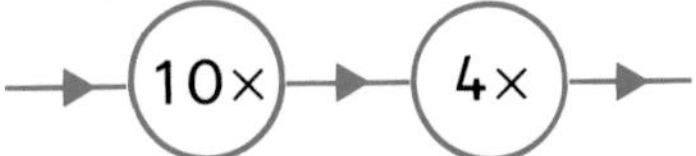

What single machine would do the same job? Check your answer by using the same numbers as in question 1.

B

We are going to use a calculator to find factors of larger numbers.
Remember, 2 is a factor of 36 because 36 ÷ 2 works out exactly with no remainder.

1. Using squared paper, make a table like this.
Tick the factors shown in the table that you find for each number.

	Factors									
Number	1	2	3	4	5	6	8	9	10	12
36		✓								
60										
48										
96										
72										
120										
90										
360										

2. Here are some numbers which have two other factors apart from themselves and 1.
Find the four factors each time, e.g. 55 — *factors are 1, 5, 11, 55*

(a) 91 (b) 57 (c) 133
(d) 221 (e) 65 (f) 187
(g) 209 (h) 247 (i) 323

Hint: some of the factors are bigger than 12. You will need your calculator!

Dotty Patterns 6 ■ 21

A

You will need a calculator.

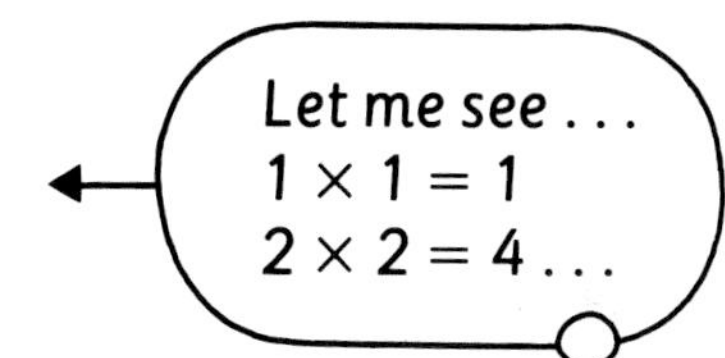

1. Make a list of the first twenty square numbers like this:

   1 ⟶ 4 ⟶ 9 ⟶ 16 ⟶ 25 ⟶

2. Now find the difference between one square number and the next.

   $1 \xrightarrow{+3} 4 \xrightarrow{+5} 9 \xrightarrow{+7} 16 \longrightarrow$

   What pattern can you see?
   Use the pattern to make two more square numbers by adding on.

3. Captain Dotty has found some special square numbers:

9	+	16	=	25		36	+	64	=	100
square number		square number		square number		square number		square number		square number

   Can you find two square numbers which add up to

   (a) 169? (b) 289?

4. We say that 19 × 19 is 19 squared. Use your calculator to find:

   (a) 24 squared (b) 33 squared (c) 41 squared (d) 37 squared

B

You will need some squared paper.

1. Draw these triangular numbers on your squared paper.

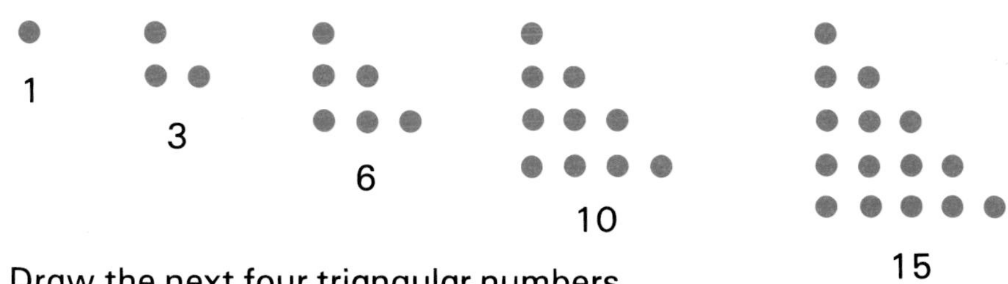

2. Draw the next four triangular numbers.
3. Copy and complete:

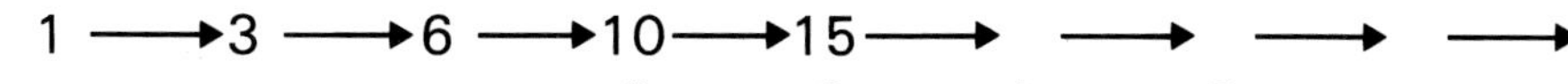

4. Copy this pattern: $1 \xrightarrow{+2} 3 \xrightarrow{+3} 6 \xrightarrow{+4} 10 \xrightarrow{+5} 15 \longrightarrow$

   Continue the pattern until you have found twenty triangular numbers.

5. Draw a circle around every triangular number that is even, like this:

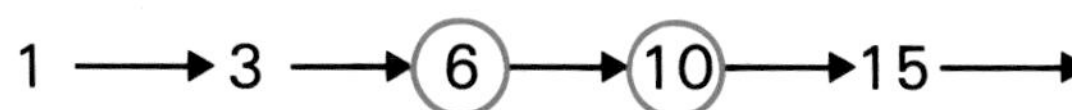

   Write about the pattern.

A

You will need some squared paper and a red and a blue pencil.
You will also need the worksheet called Machine Records and a calculator.

1. Use a red pencil to draw these triangular numbers on squared paper.

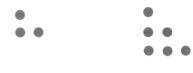

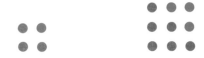

Now use a blue pencil to turn them into square numbers.

2. What shapes do the blue dots make?
3. Do the same for the next four triangular numbers. Is the pattern the same for the blue dots?
4. Make a table like this to show the pattern. Write about the pattern in the difference column.

Triangular number	Square number	Difference
1	1	0
3	4	1
6	9	3
210	400	

5. Put the first 10 triangular numbers into this double machine. Use your calculator to help.

What do you notice?

B

You will need a calculator.

We can find cube numbers without using cubes.

Look: $2 \times 2 \times 2 = 8$
We say: "2 cubed is 8."

Also: $3 \times 3 \times 3 = 27$
We say: "3 cubed is 27."

1. Copy and continue.
Use your calculator to help.

1 cubed is $1 \times 1 \times 1 =$
2 cubed is $2 \times 2 \times 2 = 8$
3 cubed is $3 \times 3 \times 3 = 27$
4 cubed is $4 \times 4 \times 4 =$
5 cubed is

Go as far as 20 cubed.

2. Can you see any patterns in the units digits of the cube numbers?

You will need the worksheet called Machine Records and a calculator.

A

1. This is a double machine.

Fill in a table for it.

In	Middle	Out
4	12	24
2		
3		
5		
1		

2. Here is a single machine.

Put the numbers from question 1 into it and fill in a table.

The new machine does the same job as the double machine but it is quicker.

B

Here are some more double machines.

Machine A → ×5 → ×2 →

Machine B → ×2 → ×4 →

Machine C → ×3 → ×3 →

Machine D → ×4 → ×2 →

1. Put 1, 2 and 3 into each machine in turn and fill in a table each time.
2. Which two machines do the same work? Why?
3. Which single machine can replace:
   (a) Machine A? (c) Machine C?
   (b) Machine B? (d) Machine D?
4. Check your single machines by putting 1, 2 and 3 into each one. Fill in a table each time.
5. Find a single machine to replace:

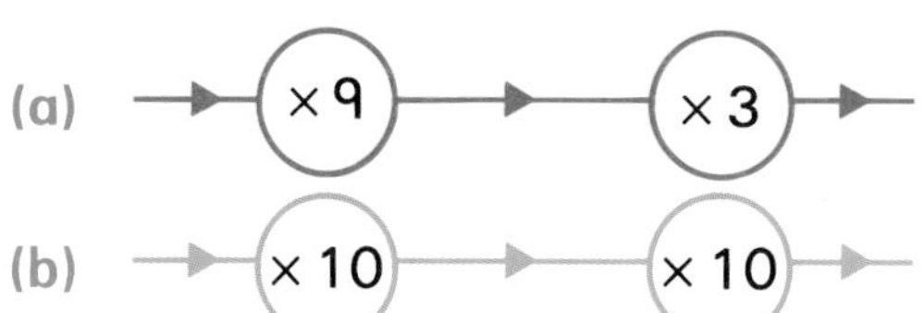

C

This double machine does the same job as this single machine.

Find a double machine to replace each of these:

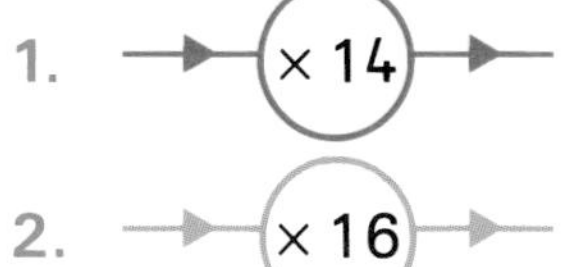

3. → ×15 →
4. → ×18 →
5. → ×50 →
6. → ×100 →
7. Now find a different double machine for each one.

More Chains

A

You will need a counter to move along the flow chart.

1. Look at this flow chart. Find out what happens to all numbers up to 50.
2. Write about what happens to multiples of 3.
3. Write about what happens to other numbers.

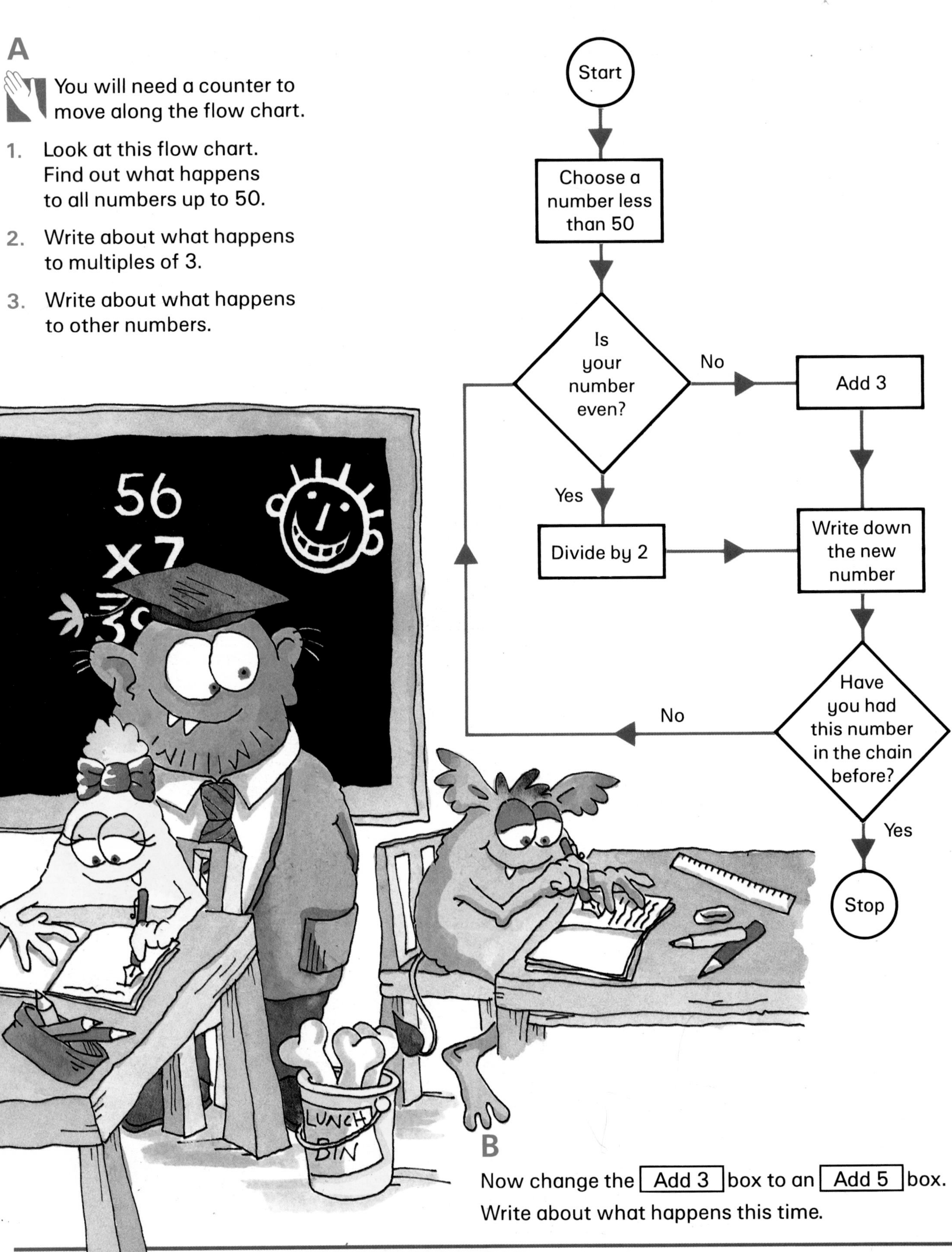
Start
Choose a number less than 50
Is your number even?
No
Add 3
Yes
Divide by 2
Write down the new number
Have you had this number in the chain before?
No
Yes
Stop
56
x 7
LUNCH BIN

B

Now change the **Add 3** box to an **Add 5** box.
Write about what happens this time.

Sort The Shapes

You will need the worksheet called Quadrilaterals and the one called Sorting Boxes. Work with a friend.

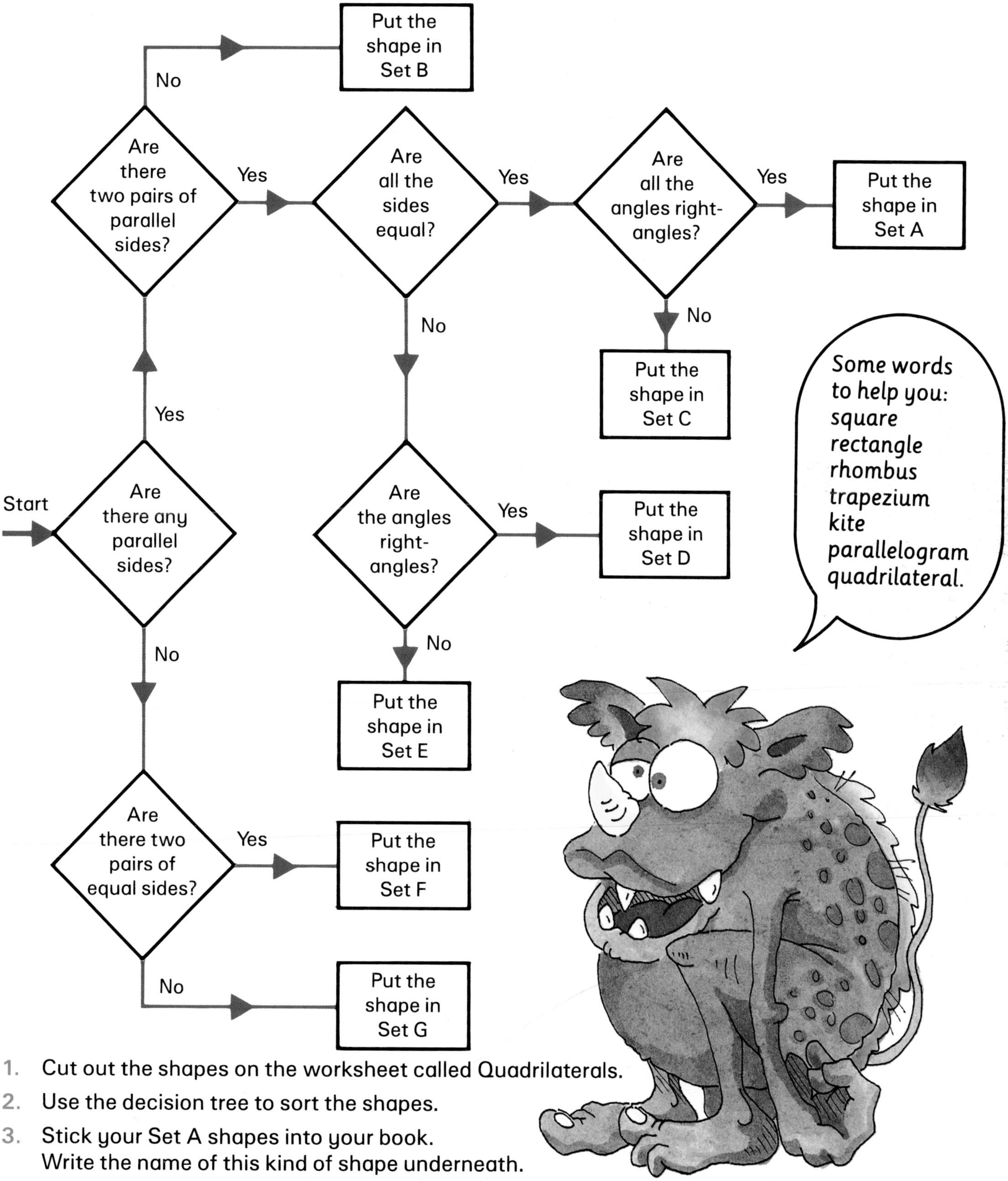

Start

Are there any parallel sides?

Yes → Are there two pairs of parallel sides?

No → Put the shape in Set B

Yes → Are all the sides equal?

Yes → Are all the angles right-angles?

Yes → Put the shape in Set A

No → Put the shape in Set C

No → Are the angles right-angles?

Yes → Put the shape in Set D

No → Put the shape in Set E

No → Are there two pairs of equal sides?

Yes → Put the shape in Set F

No → Put the shape in Set G

Some words to help you:
square
rectangle
rhombus
trapezium
kite
parallelogram
quadrilateral.

1. Cut out the shapes on the worksheet called Quadrilaterals.
2. Use the decision tree to sort the shapes.
3. Stick your Set A shapes into your book.
   Write the name of this kind of shape underneath.
4. Do the same for all the other sets of shapes.

You will need some squared paper.

A

Wesley is raising money towards a new school minibus.
He has made a new kind of ready reckoner to help him work out the cost of raffle tickets.
Each ticket costs 20p.

1. Copy and complete this table:

Number of tickets	1	2	4	8
Cost in pence	20			

2. Look at this graph. What does each step on the cost axis stand for?

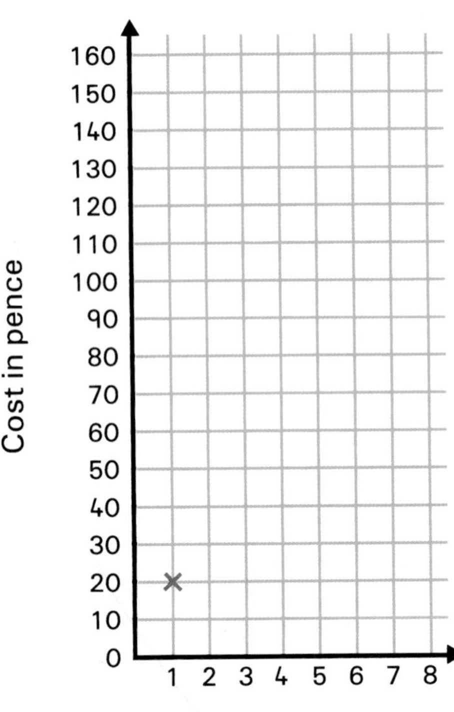

3. (a) Copy this graph.
   (b) Plot all the costs in your table onto your graph.
   (c) Using a ruler, join all the crosses with a straight line.

4. (a) What is the cost of 3 raffle tickets?
   (b) What is the cost of 6 raffle tickets?
   (c) Plot these costs on your graph. What do you notice?

B

Next, Wesley worked out the cost of tickets for the tombola stall. Each ticket costs 25p.

1. Copy and complete this table.

Number of tickets	1	4	8
Cost in pence	25		

2. (a) Draw a graph like the one in Part A, but this time use 1 step for 25p on the vertical axis.
   (b) Now plot all the costs in your table onto your graph.
   (c) Using a ruler, join all the crosses with a straight line.

3. (a) What is the cost of 2 tombola tickets?
   (b) What is the cost of 6 tombola tickets?
   (c) Plot these costs on your graph. What do you notice?

4. Use the graph to find the cost of 5 tombola tickets.

Holiday Spending

You will need a calculator.

A

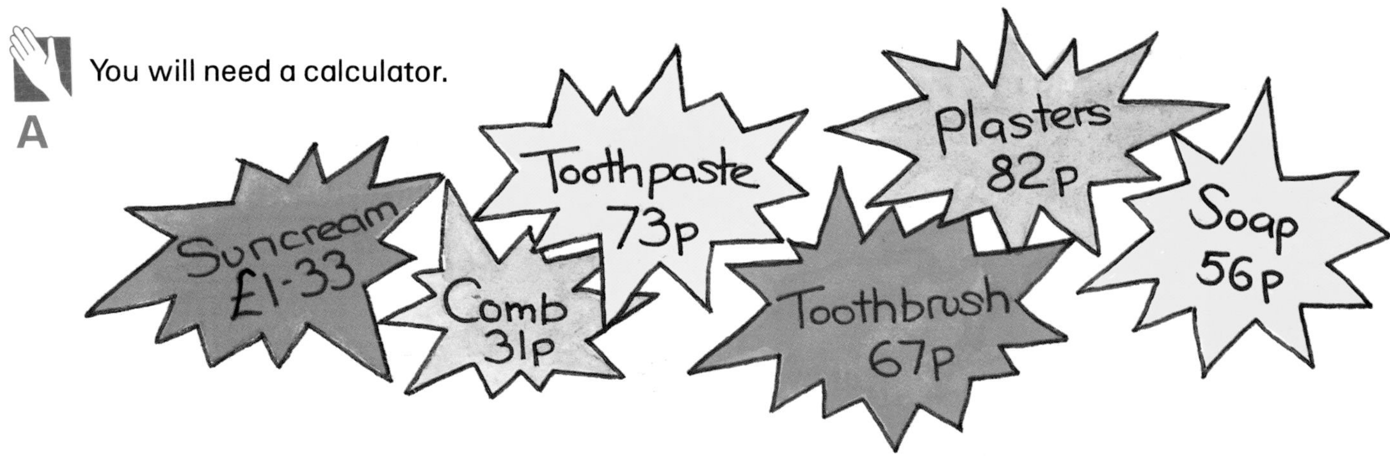

Write out and total each holiday shopping bill.

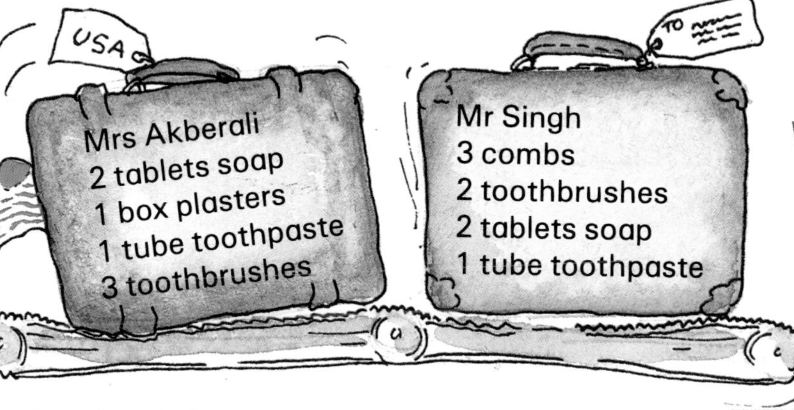

USA
Mrs Akberali
2 tablets soap
1 box plasters
1 tube toothpaste
3 toothbrushes
Mr Singh
3 combs
2 toothbrushes
2 tablets soap
1 tube toothpaste

Miss Baker
3 tablets soap
1 box plasters
2 bottles suncream
2 toothbrushes

Mr Hughes
1 tablet soap
1 toothbrush
1 comb
1 bottle suncream

1. Which 3 customers could pay with £5?
   How much change would each get?
2. Who spent most? Who spent least?
3. How much did the 4 customers spend altogether?

B

1. 3 souvenir pens cost £2·85. How much will 9 pens cost?
2. (a) How many badges at 11p each can I buy for £5?
   (b) What will my change be?
3. Petrol costs 46p for a litre. How much will $5\frac{1}{2}$ litres cost?
4. Mr and Mrs Upton take their 4 children to the safari park on the coach.
   They all have a meal. How much does the trip cost?

Coach
Adults: £4·50
Children: £3·00

Safari Park
Adults: £2·75
Children: £1·50

Dinner
Adults: £2·50
Children: £1·65

5. Mrs Bridges takes her 6 children on the same trip.
   How much more/less than Mr and Mrs Upton does Mrs Bridges spend?

A

You will need a ruler.

Here is a plan of the Giant Market at Bigtown. 1cm on the plan means 1m at the market.

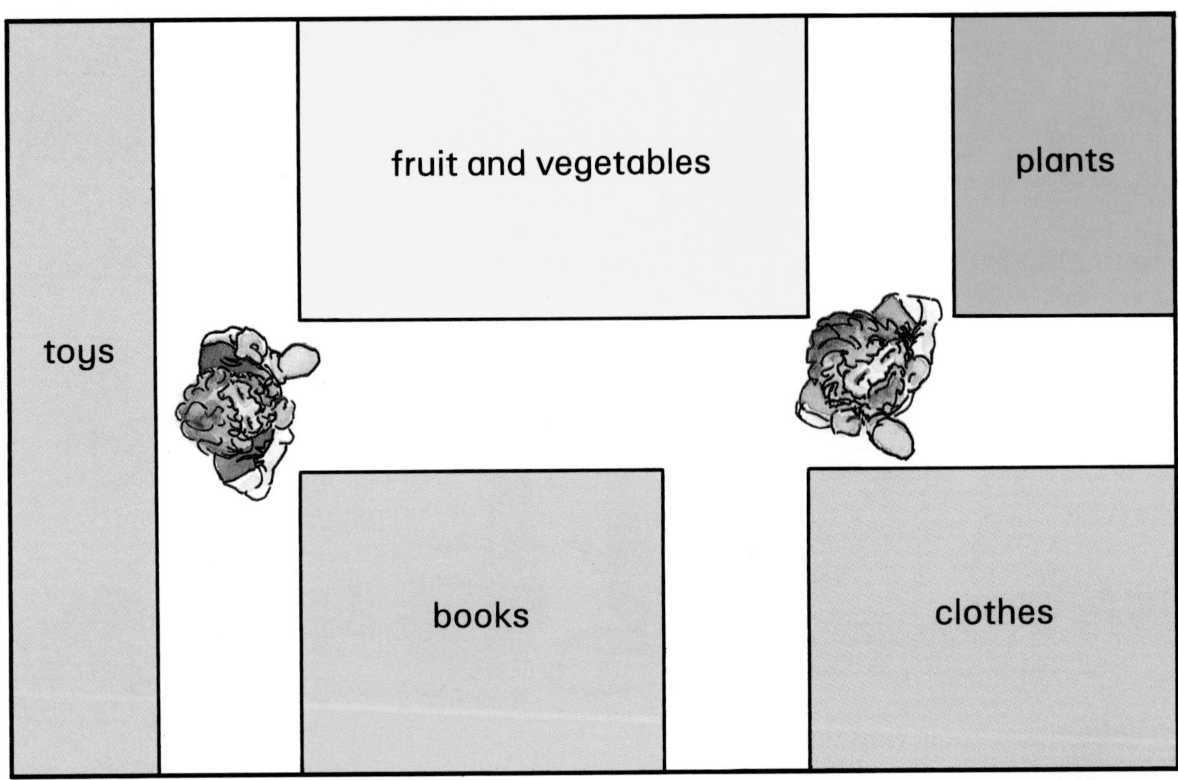

Read these questions carefully and measure the plan to work out the answers.

1. How long is the market on the plan?
2. How long is the real Giant Market?
3. How wide are the paths on the plan?
4. How wide are the paths in the real market?
5. Measure each stall and write down in your book:
   (a) the size of the stall on the plan
   (b) what its length and width would be in the real market.

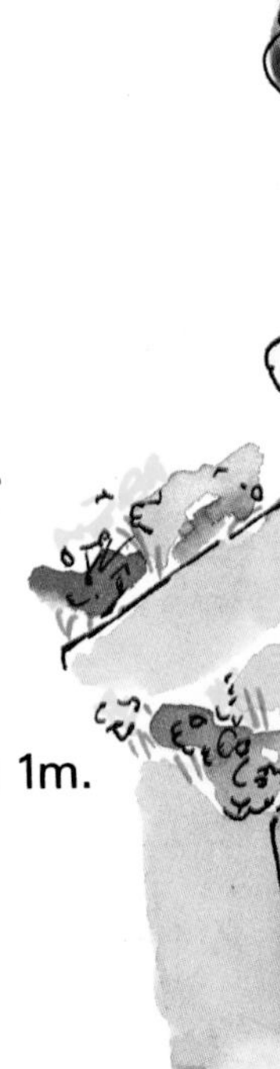

B

You will need a ruler and some centimetre squared paper.

Draw a plan for each of these new stalls. Use 1cm to represent 1m.

1. The flower stall is 6m long and $2\frac{1}{2}$m wide.
2. The cake stall is 3m 50cm wide and 5m long.
3. The stationery stall is square. It is $4\frac{1}{2}$m wide.
4. The bric-a-brac stall is twice as long as it is wide. It is 4m long.

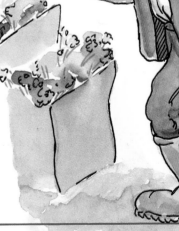

You will need a ruler.

Here is a map showing the Giant's territory.
He always walks along the same straight footpath from one place to another.
On this map 1cm represents 1km in real distances.

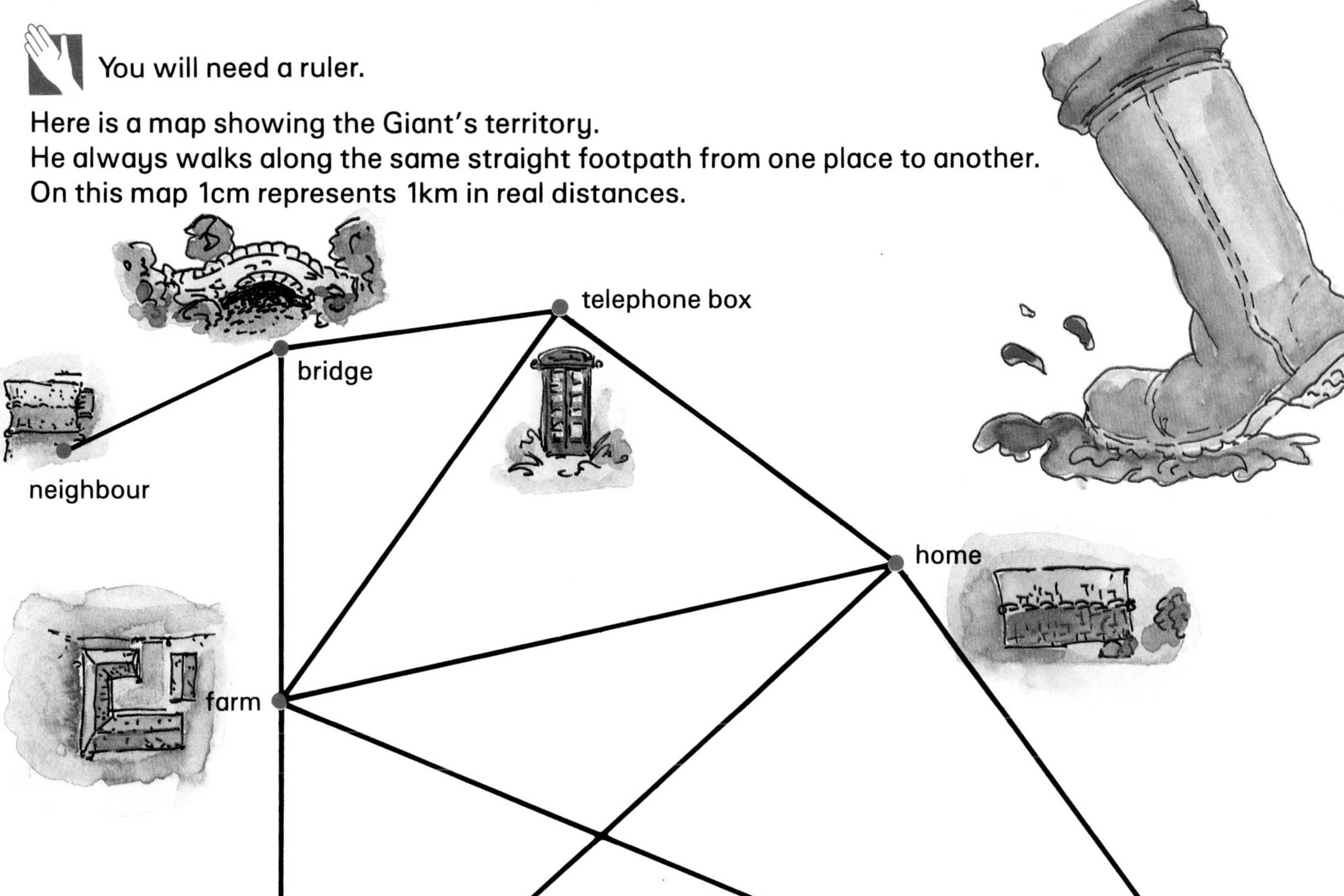

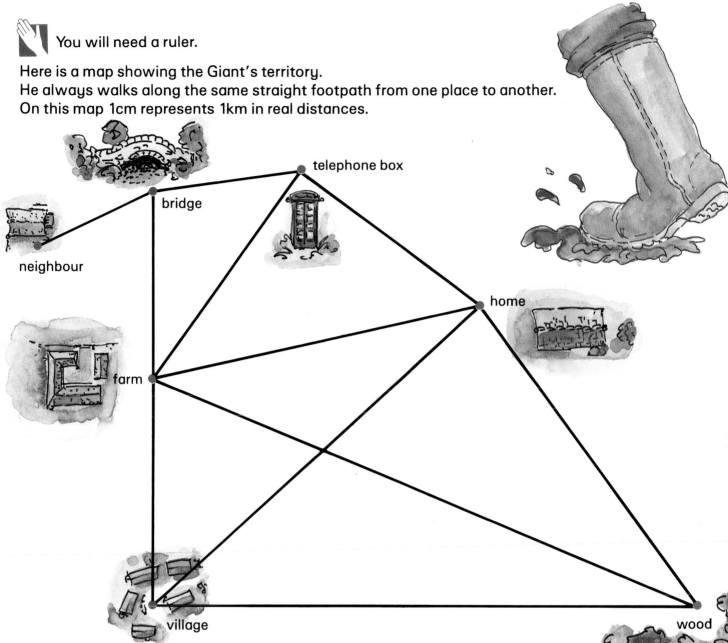

1. Copy and complete this table. Always use the shortest route.

Journey	Distance on map	Real distance
home to the wood		
village to the farm		
farm to the wood		
home to the bridge		
village to home		
home to neighbour		

2. Once a week the Giant visits all the places in his territory, including his neighbour's house.
   (a) How far does he walk?
   (b) Can you find a shorter route?

A

You will need a ruler.

Farmer Frank's garden is 22 metres long and 10 metres wide.
Here is a plan of it.

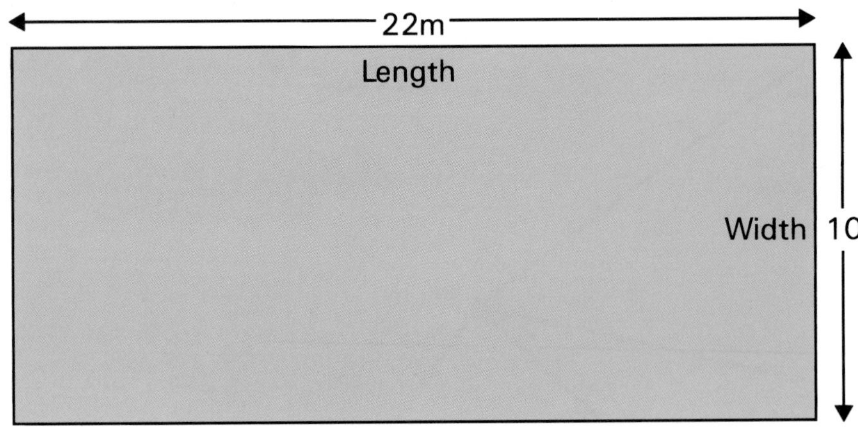

1. How many centimetres long is the plan?
2. How many centimetres wide is the plan?
3. Copy and complete these sentences:

   5cm on the plan is ____m in real life.
   ____cm on the plan is 2m in real life.
   The scale of the plan is 1cm to ____m.

B

You will need a ruler and some centimetre squared paper.

Farmer Frank has a field of cows with a milking shed and barn in it.

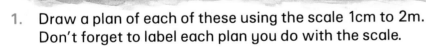

1. Draw a plan of each of these using the scale 1cm to 2m. Don't forget to label each plan you do with the scale.
   (a) A barn measuring 26m long and 14m wide.
   (b) A milking shed measuring 18m long and 9m wide.
2. Another field is 110m long and 75m wide. Draw a plan of it using the scale 1cm to 10m.
3. (a) Draw the second field again this time using the scale 1cm to 5m.
   (b) Does it look the same as the one you drew for question 2, or does it look different?

You will need a ruler.

A

Here are two maps of a cycle race. The race starts and finishes at Wheelville.
The scales of the maps are different.

1. Use Map A to answer these questions.
   Measure to the nearest centimetre.
   (a) How many kilometres do the cyclists cover from Start to Biker's Hill?
   (b) How far have they cycled when they reach Saddler's Stop?
   (c) Which is the longest part of the course?
   (d) How far is the whole race?
   (e) One cyclist gets a puncture at Saddler's Stop. He takes the short cut to Wheelville. How far does he have to walk?

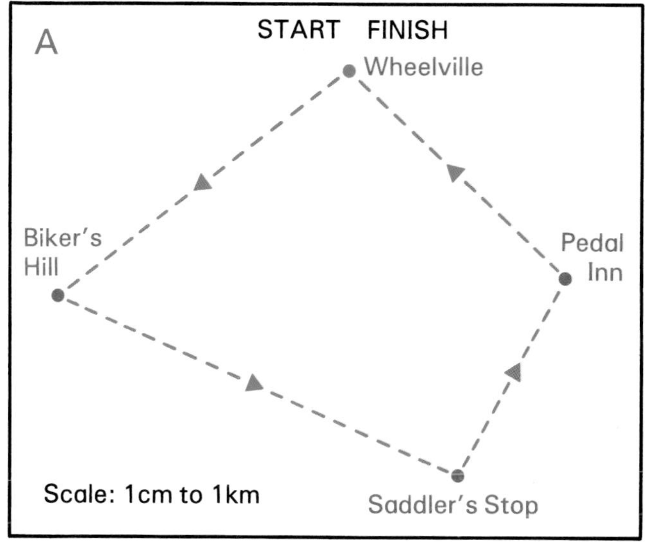

2. Now answer the same questions from Map B.
3. Are your answers the same for both maps?
   Why? Talk to your teacher about this.

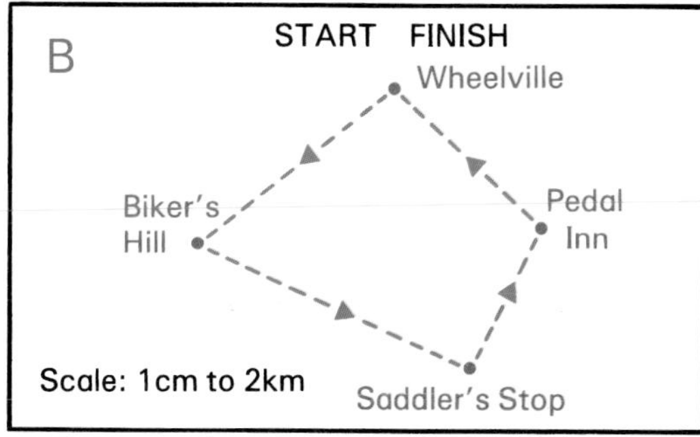

B

This is a scale drawing of an air-sea rescue.
The scale is 1cm to 5km.

Key: ● helicopter x trawler

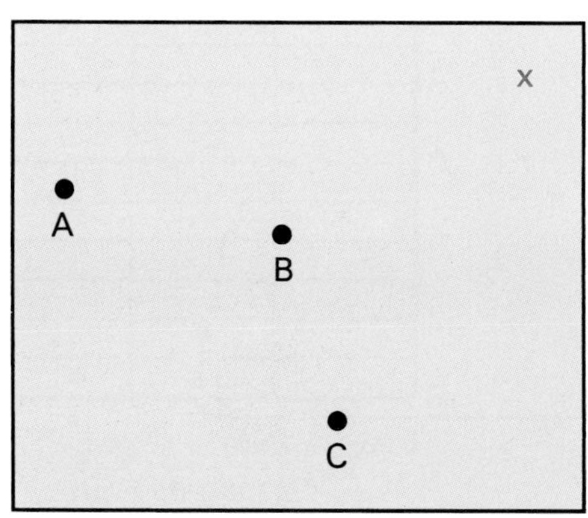

1. How far from the trawler is:
   (a) helicopter A?
   (b) helicopter B?
   (c) helicopter C?
2. Helicopter B has engine trouble.
   Helicopter C goes to help it.
   How far does helicopter C have to travel?
3. Helicopter A is travelling at 10km every hour.
   The trawler can keep afloat for another $2\frac{1}{2}$ hours. Can helicopter A get there in time?

A

Alan has drawn this graph to show what time he and his friends go to bed. Look at it carefully.

1. At what time does Alan go to bed?
2. Who goes to bed one hour later than Sam?
3. At what time does Reena go to bed?
4. How long has Jim been in bed if it is now 11pm?
5. How many of Alan's friends go to bed earlier than he does?
6. Alan and his friends get up at 8am. Who has been in bed for the longest time?
7. Now make a bedtime graph for six of your friends.

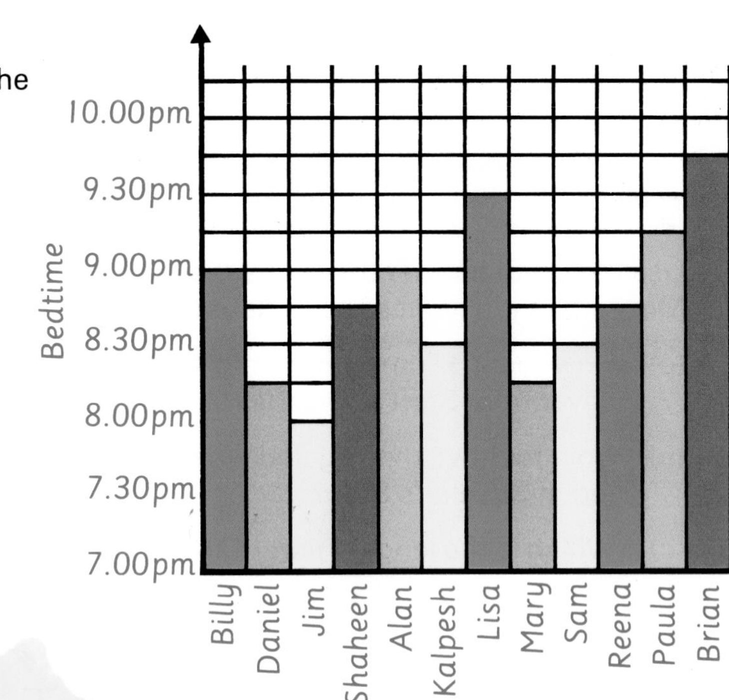

B

You will need some squared paper.

Alan asked all the children what time they got up on a Saturday morning. This is what he found.

Time	Tally
7.00am	|
7.15am	||
7.30am	𝍸
7.45am	𝍸 |
8.00am	||||
8.15am	|
8.30am	|
8.45am	||
9.00am	|

In here we put all the children who get up between 8 and 9, including those who get up at 8, but not those who get up at 9.

Use this information to draw a graph. Set it out like this:

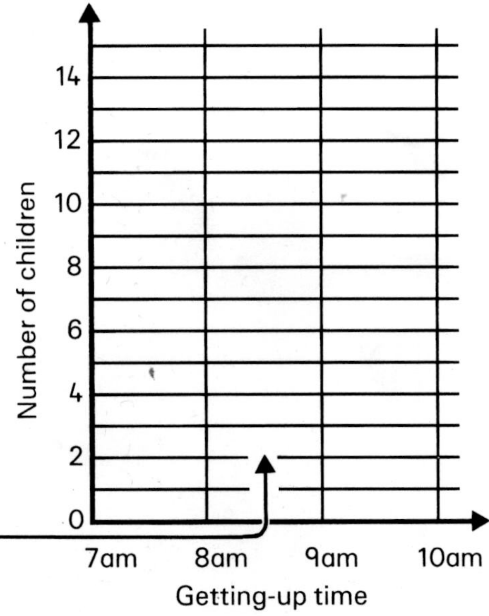

A

Here are some times shown on digital watches.

22:00 15:36 17:02 11:51 8:56 17:59

Which digital watch time matches which sentence?

1. It's nearly 9 o'clock.
2. It's just after half past 3.
3. It's just gone 5 o'clock.
4. It's nearly lunchtime.
5. It's about 6 o'clock.
6. It's time you were in bed!

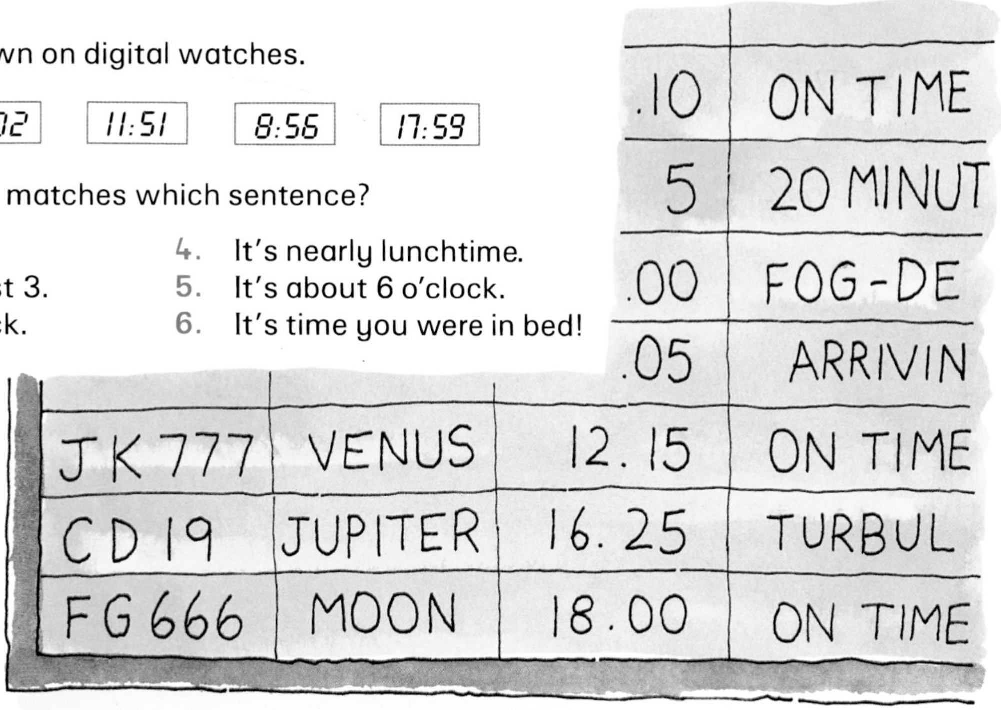

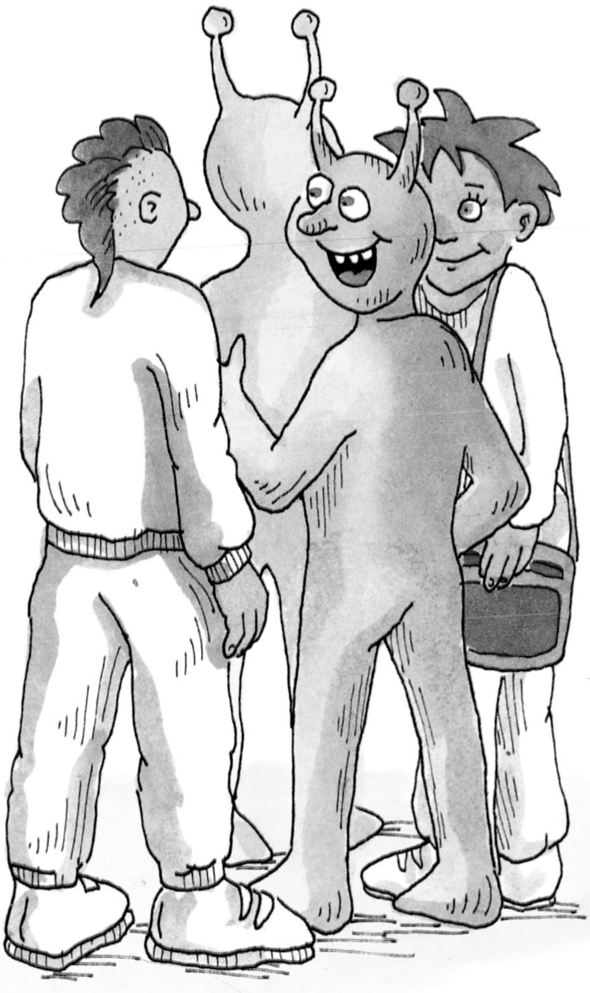

B

Copy and complete the sentences.

1. If it is 13:30 now, 25 minutes ago it was ____.
2. If it is 14:10 now, in 35 minutes it will be ____.
3. If it will be 18:15 in half an hour, it is ____ now.
4. It was 19:25 half an hour ago, it is ____ now.

Now complete these for yourself.

5. At 21:30 today, I will be ________.
6. At 13:15 on Sundays, I am usually ________.
7. I came to school at ____ this morning and I will go home at ____.
8. At about 16:00 yesterday, I was ________.

C

Here is part of a space station notice-board:

Flight	From	Due	Message
AB104	Mars	06.10	On time
XY92	Pluto	08.05	20 minutes late
PQ215	Earth	10.45	Fog – delayed 5 hours
ST234	Saturn	14.00	Arriving 5 mins early

Write down the time at which each flight is expected to arrive.

Counting Time 6 25

A

To find how long it is from 10.40 to 13.55 we can count on.

10.40 —3 hrs→ 13.40 —15 mins→ 13.55

Total time is 3 hours 15 minutes.

Work out how long it is between the following times:

1. 09.25 to 11.10
2. 08.45 to 10.05
3. 20.15 to 22.00
4. 19.35 to 21.20
5. 13.24 to 17.50
6. 11.05 to 13.10
7. 10.45 to 14.25
8. 11.27 to 15.05
9. 09.21 to 13.15
10. 10.17 to 16.35
11. 03.12 to 15.27
12. 04.32 to 14.51

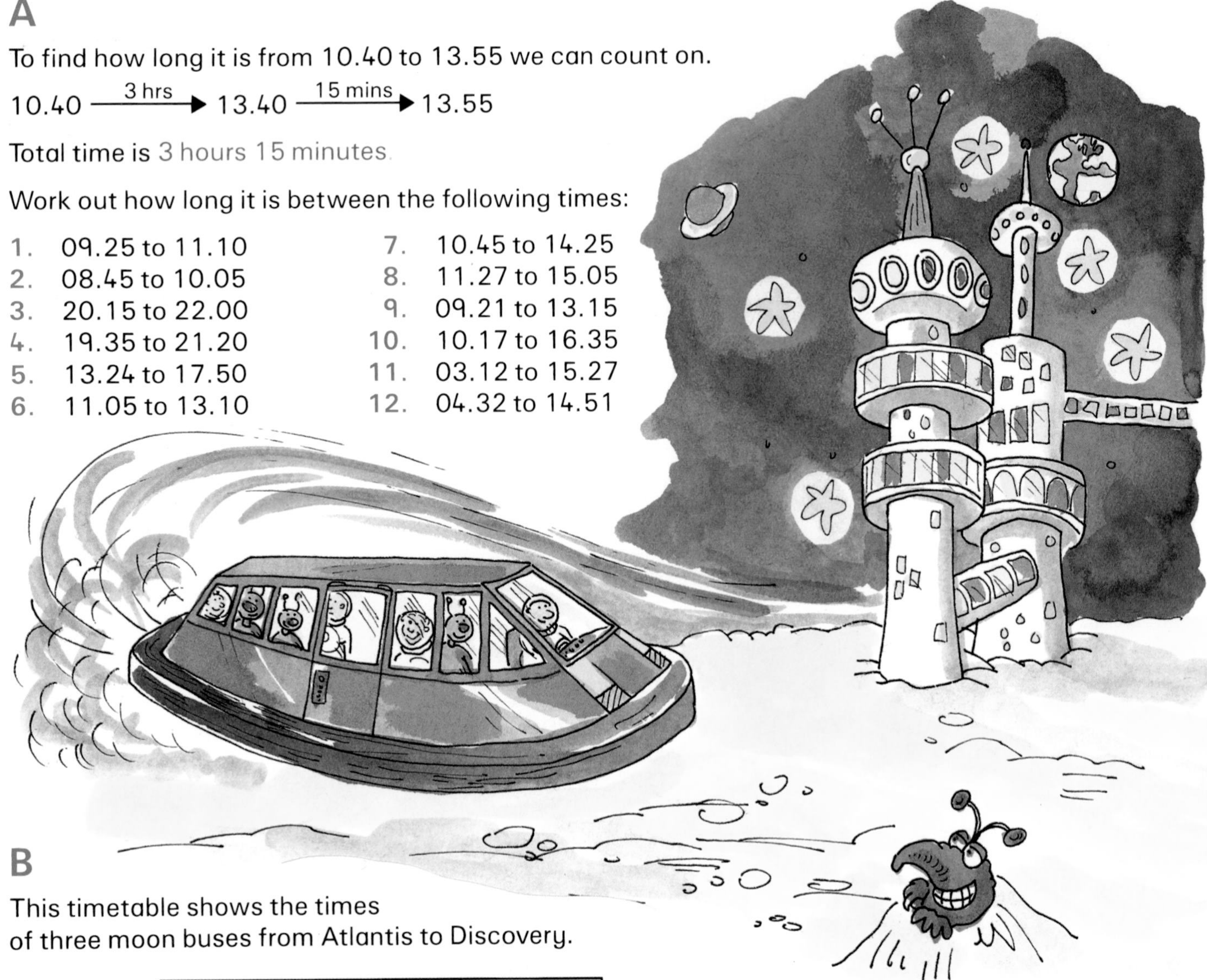

B

This timetable shows the times of three moon buses from Atlantis to Discovery.

	First bus	Second bus	Third bus
Atlantis	07.45	13.20	18.35
Challenger	08.20	13.50	19.10
Columbia	10.43	16.08	21.33
Discovery	12.51	18.13	23.45

1. How long did the first bus take to get from Atlantis to Discovery?
2. Which bus goes from Atlantis to Discovery in the shortest time?
3. Which bus arrives in Columbia just after 4.00pm?
4. How long does the third bus take to go from Atlantis to Columbia?
5. At what time does the morning bus arrive at Challenger?
6. If you just missed the first bus at Atlantis, how long would you have to wait for the next bus?
7. If you arrived at Columbia at 10.15am, how many minutes must you wait for the first bus?

A

Look at these fraction trains.

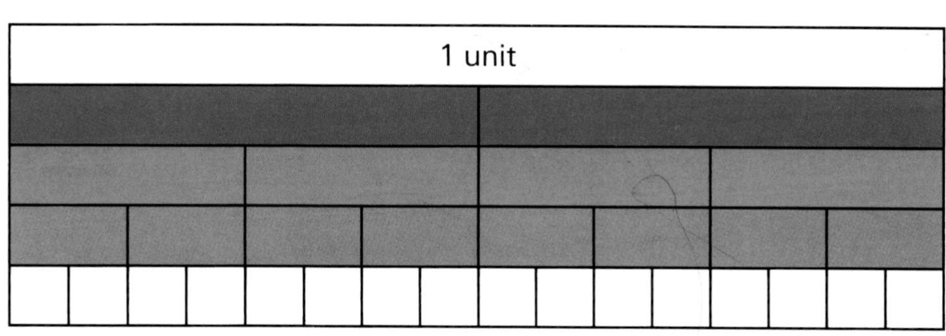

Copy and complete this sentence.

1. 2 brown rods match the unit, so the brown rod is ____ of the unit.

Now do the same for: 2. the pink rod 3. the red rod 4. the white rod

B

Look at these fraction trains.
Now the brown rod is the unit.

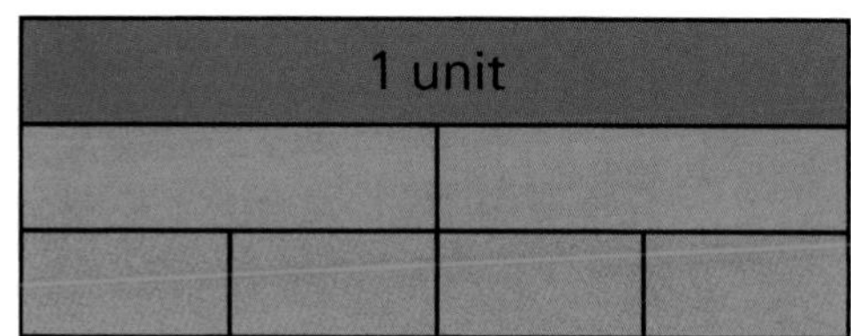

Copy and complete this sentence.

1. 2 pink rods match the brown rod, so the pink rod is ____ of the brown rod.

Now write a sentence about: 2. the red rod and the brown rod 3. the red rod and the pink rod

C

Look at these fraction trains.

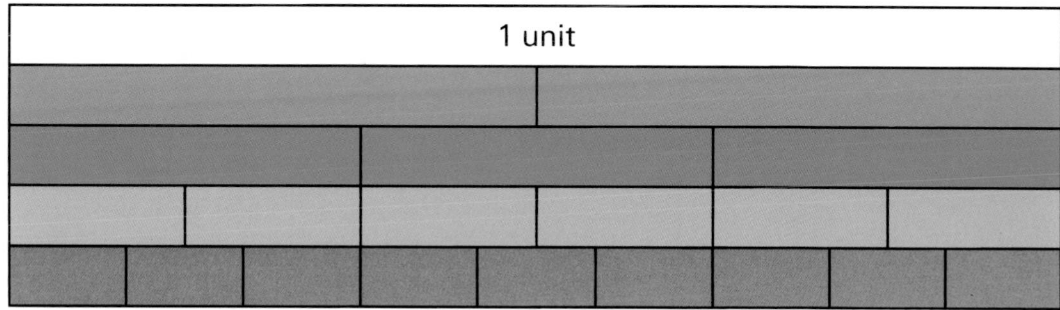

1. Write a fraction sentence about each coloured rod.

Use the fraction trains to help you find the missing fractions.

2. $\frac{1}{2} + \square = 1$ 4. $\frac{4}{6} + \square = 1$ 6. $\frac{5}{6} + \square = 1$ 8. $\frac{1}{3} + \square = 1$

3. $\frac{2}{3} + \square = 1$ 5. $\frac{2}{9} + \square = 1$ 7. $\frac{5}{9} + \square = 1$ 9. $\frac{3}{6} + \square = 1$

Coastal Fractions

A

1. $\frac{1}{3}$ of 24 = 8
2. $\frac{1}{4}$ of 24
3. $\frac{1}{6}$ of 24
4. $\frac{1}{8}$ of 24
5. $\frac{1}{12}$ of 24
6. $\frac{1}{24}$ of 24
7. $\frac{1}{3}$ of 12
8. $\frac{1}{4}$ of 16
9. $\frac{1}{5}$ of 15
10. $\frac{2}{5}$ of 15
11. $\frac{3}{4}$ of 24
12. $\frac{2}{3}$ of 12
13. $\frac{3}{8}$ of 16
14. $\frac{3}{7}$ of 14
15. $\frac{4}{9}$ of 18

B

1. Two puffins have caught 20 fish. One of them caught $\frac{1}{4}$ of the fish.
   (a) What fraction of the fish did the other puffin catch?
   (b) How many fish did each puffin catch?
2. You find 24 fossils. You find $\frac{1}{6}$ of them around the rock pools and the rest beneath the cliffs.
   (a) What fraction of them did you find beneath the cliffs?
   (b) How many fossils did you find beneath the cliffs?
3. There are 15 litter bins on the beach. $\frac{1}{5}$ of them are full.
   (a) What fraction of the litter bins are not full?
   (b) How many litter bins are full?
4. An hour ago a boat was 18km away from the coast. It has now moved $\frac{2}{3}$ of this distance towards the coast.
   (a) How far has the boat moved?
   (b) How far is it from the coast?
5. The tide is coming in, and in 36 minutes you will be cut off. You make your way across the beach, and in $\frac{4}{9}$ of this time you are halfway to safety.
   (a) How much time do you have left?
   (b) Do you think you can make it?

You will need the worksheet called Machine Records.

A

1. Fill in a table for this double machine.

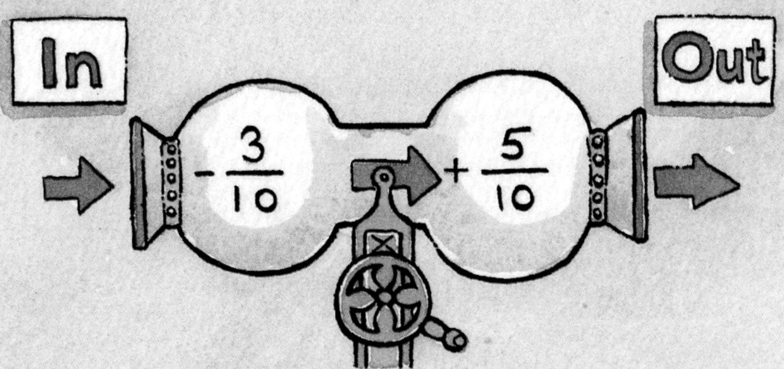

In	Middle	Out
$\frac{7}{10}$	$\frac{4}{10}$	$\frac{9}{10}$
$\frac{8}{10}$		
$\frac{5}{10}$		
$\frac{4}{10}$		

2. Fill in a table for this single machine.

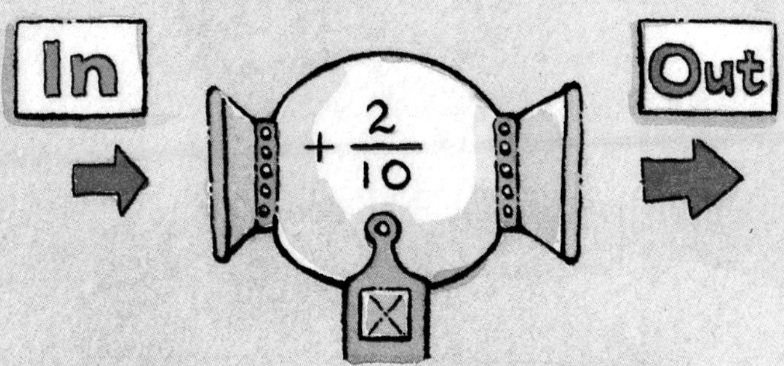

In	Out
$\frac{7}{10}$	
$\frac{8}{10}$	
$\frac{5}{10}$	
$\frac{4}{10}$	

3. What do you notice?

B

1. Fill in a table for this machine.
   Use the same numbers as question 1, Part A.

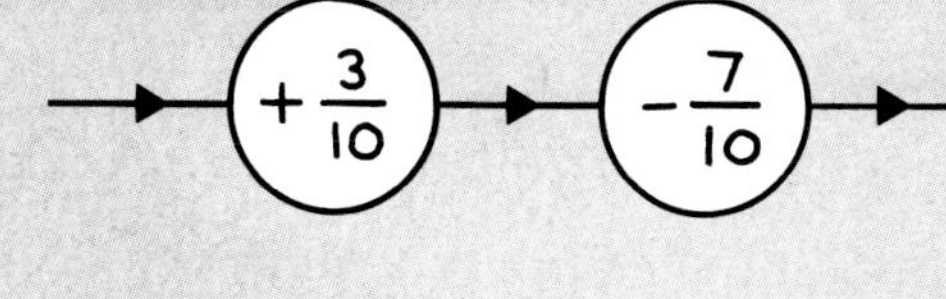

2. This single machine gives the same answers.
   What should its label say?

C

1. Fill in a table for this machine.
   Use the same numbers as question 1, Part A.

2. This single machine gives the same answers.
   What should its label say?

You will need a ruler.

A

Write down the areas of these shapes in square centimetres.

1.
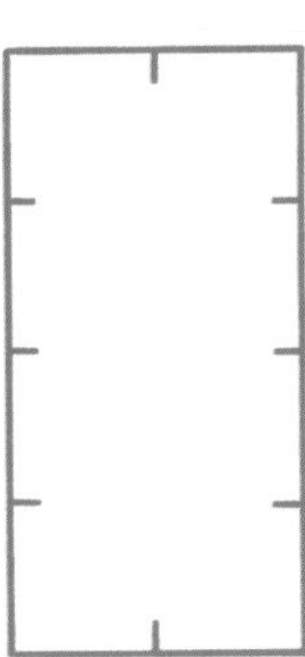

2.

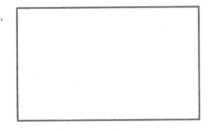

3.
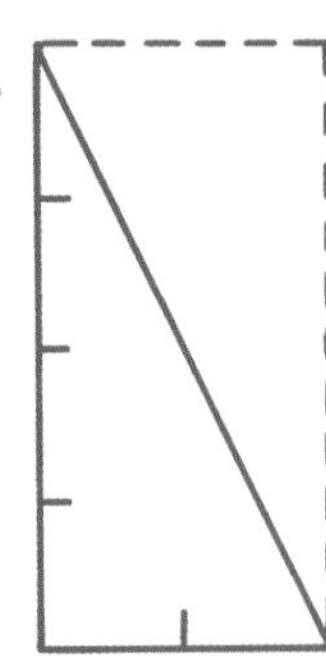

4.

5.
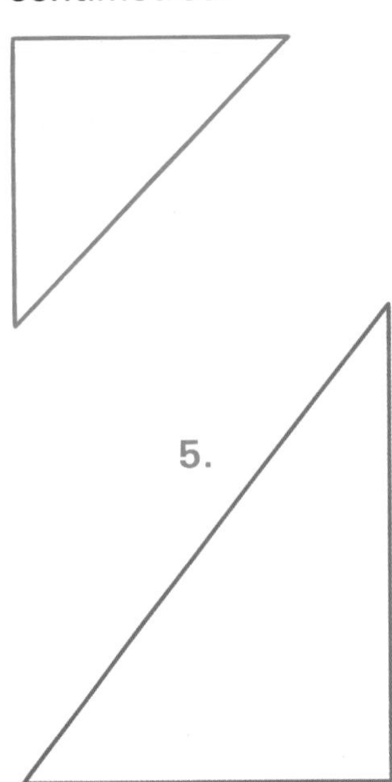

6.

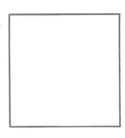

7.
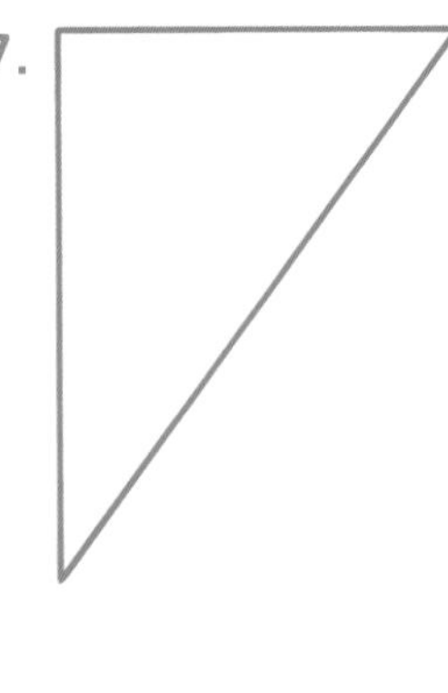

B

Now try these shapes. You will need to split them into rectangles and triangles.

1.

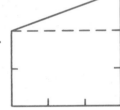

2.
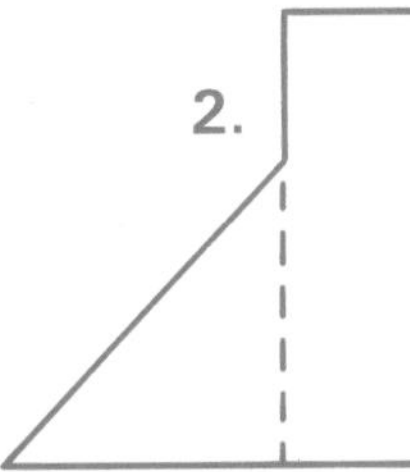

3.
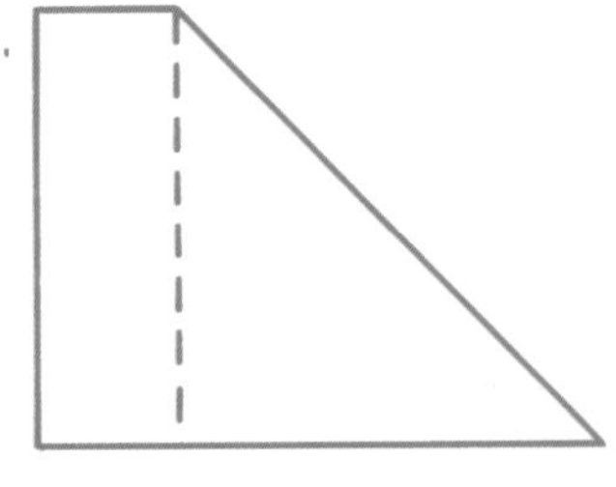

4.
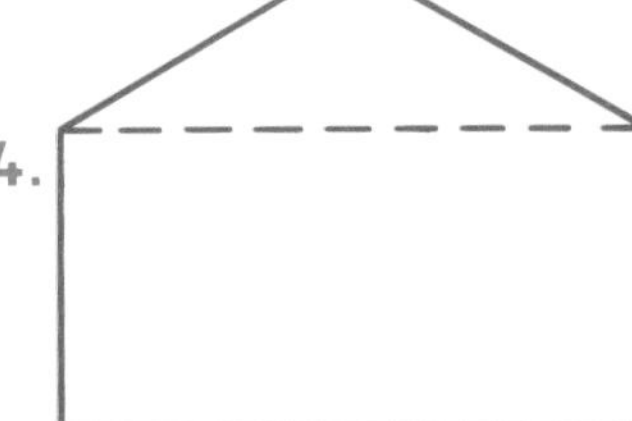

C

Joni has a piece of squared centimetre paper like this →

What area of the paper is left when she has cut out these four shapes?

Find the area of each shape first.

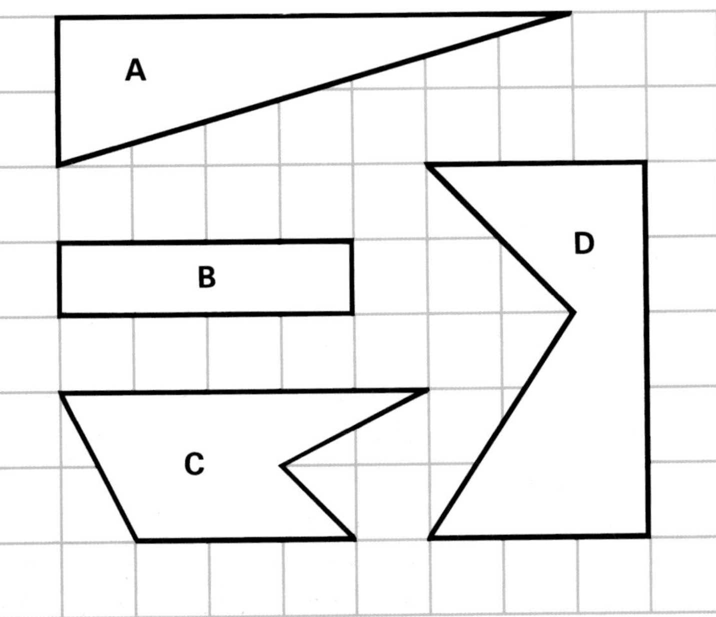

Enlarge The Shapes

You will need some squared paper and a ruler.

A

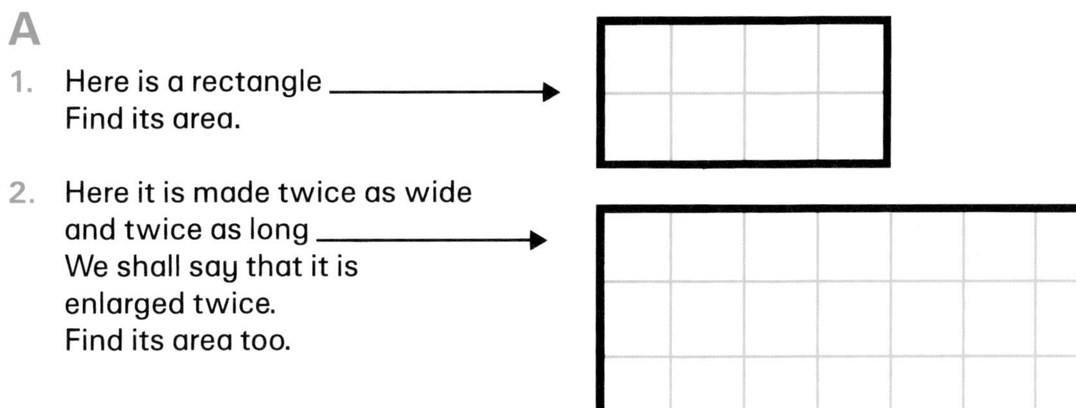

1. Here is a rectangle →
   Find its area.
2. Here it is made twice as wide and twice as long →
   We shall say that it is enlarged twice.
   Find its area too.
3. Draw the small rectangle from question 1 on your squared paper.
   Now make each side three times the size of the first one.
   We say it is enlarged three times. Find its area.
4. Now enlarge the rectangle four times and find its area.
5. Write about any patterns you can see.

B

Here is a shape →

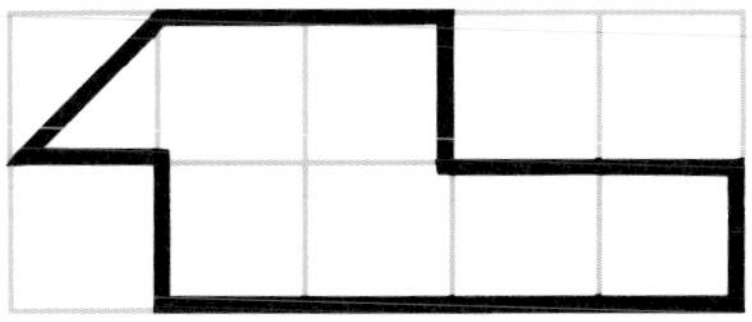

Here it is enlarged twice →

Each side is twice as big.

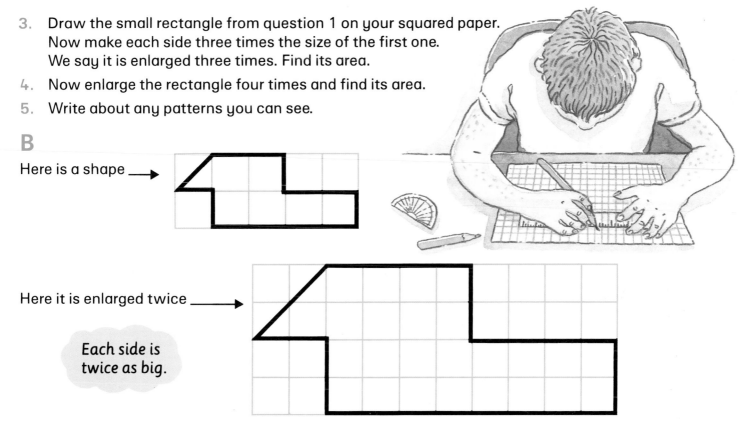

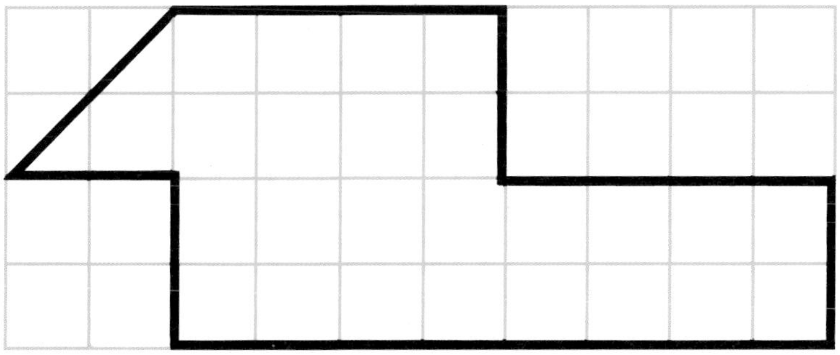

1. Find the area of each shape.
2. Draw the shape enlarged three times and four times on squared paper.
   Find the area of each shape.
3. Write about the pattern this time.
   Is it the same as the pattern in Part A?
4. Now draw any other shape made of squares and half-squares.
   Then draw it enlarged twice, three times and four times.

Measure The Maze

You will need an Area Grid or a ruler to help you.

Here is a plan of a new maze. Each centimetre represents one metre.

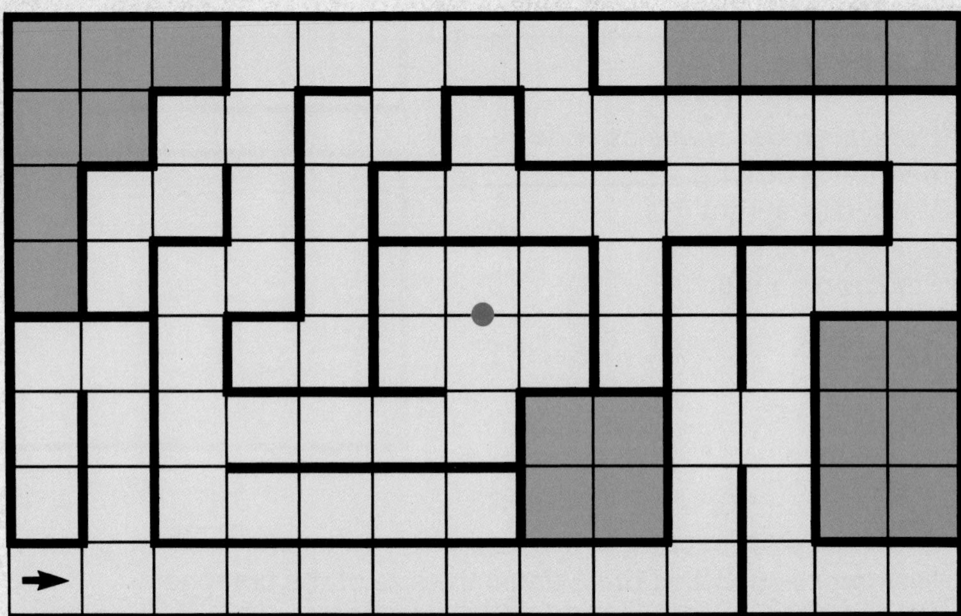

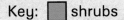

1. What is the total area of the ground taken up by the maze?
2. Shrubs will be planted in the shaded parts. How many shrubs will be needed if they plant three shrubs in every square metre?
3. How many square metres of grass turf will they need for the paths?
4. Turf costs £1·50 per square metre. How much will it cost to turf the paths?
5. They plan to grow a tall hedge round the outside of the maze. The hedge needs four plants for every metre of its length. How many plants do they need?
6. About how far would you walk if you went straight to the centre?
7. Design a maze of your own and give it to a friend to try.

A

Look at these units, tenths and hundredths drawn on squared paper.

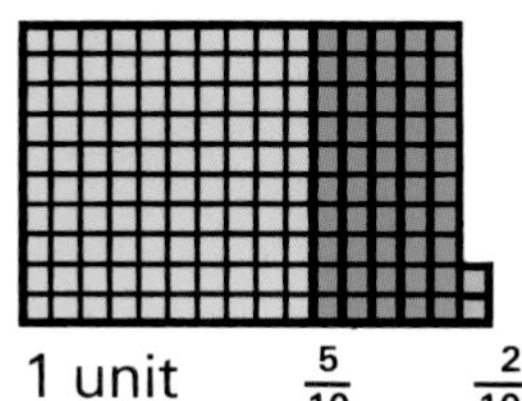

They would look like this on a counting board →

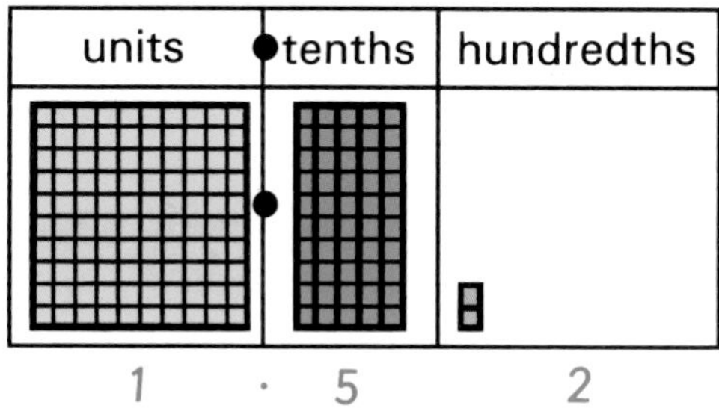

Write these as decimals. The first one is done for you.

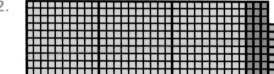

1. *1 unit, 9 tenths, 3 hundredths → 1·93*
2.
3.
4.
5.
6. 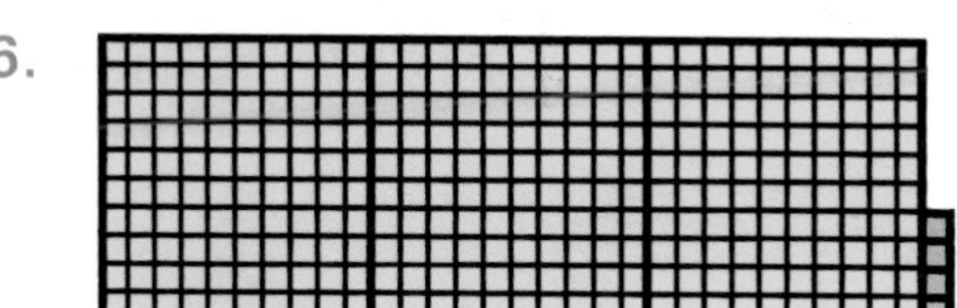
7.
8.

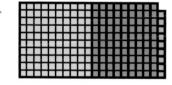

B

You will need some squared paper.
Colour these on your squared paper.

1. 4·86
2. 3·29
3. 2·78
4. 5·15
5. 3·50
6. 4·07
7. 0·54
8. 0·60
9. 0·01
10. 4·88
11. Half of 4·88
12. Quarter of 4·88

Metres And Decimals

A

This is a 10cm rod.

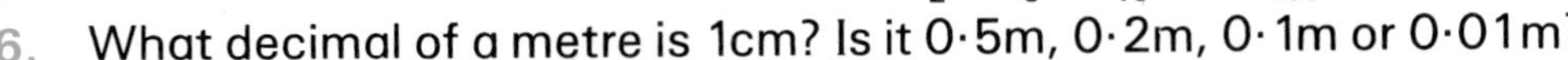

Write the answers in your book.

1. How many 10cm rods, laid end to end, would be needed to measure 1m?
2. How many 1cm rods, laid end to end, would be needed to measure 100cm?
3. What fraction of a metre is 10cm? Is it $\frac{1}{2}$m, $\frac{1}{5}$m, $\frac{1}{10}$m or $\frac{1}{100}$m?
4. What decimal of a metre is 10cm? Is it 0·5m, 0·2m, 0·1m or 0·01m?
5. What fraction of a metre is 1cm? Is it $\frac{1}{2}$m, $\frac{1}{5}$m, $\frac{1}{10}$m or $\frac{1}{100}$m?
6. What decimal of a metre is 1cm? Is it 0·5m, 0·2m, 0·1m or 0·01m?

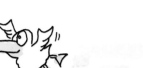

B

A plank is 1m and 20cm long.
We can write: $1\frac{2}{10}$m
or we can use decimals and write: 1·20m or 1·2m

A rope is 2m and 25cm long.
We can write: 2m and $\frac{2}{10}$m and $\frac{5}{100}$m
or we can use decimals and write: 2·25m

Copy these into your book and then write them in metres using decimals.

1. 1m and 10cm
2. 5m and 62cm
3. 10m and 45cm
4. 3m and 3cm
5. 76cm
6. 8cm

C

1. A piece of wood is 1·30m long. If you cut it into 10cm pieces, how many pieces would you have?
2. A counter is 0·01m across. How many counters would we need to put in a line to make it 2m long?
3. Which is the largest measurement: 424cm, 4·03m or $4\frac{3}{10}$m?

You will need a decimal number line.

A

Use your number line to help you do these.

1.	0·4 + 0·7	5.	0·9 + 0·7	9.	1·4 + 0·2
2.	1·2 + 0·5	6.	0·8 + 0·6	10.	1·5 + 1·1
3.	0·7 + 0·9	7.	0·5 + 0·7	11.	1·4 + 0·8
4.	1·3 + 0·4	8.	1·0 + 0·3	12.	0·8 + 1·4

B

Now try these. Use your number line to help you again.

1.	2·3 + 0·6	5.	4·6 + 1·2	9.	0·6 + 0·7 + 0·2
2.	5·4 + 0·7	6.	3·5 + 1·4	10.	0·4 + 0·5 + 0·6
3.	6·0 + 0·9	7.	5·9 + 1·6	11.	0·8 + 0·4 + 1·1
4.	3·8 + 0·5	8.	1·9 + 1·8	12.	0·5 + 0·2 + 1·4

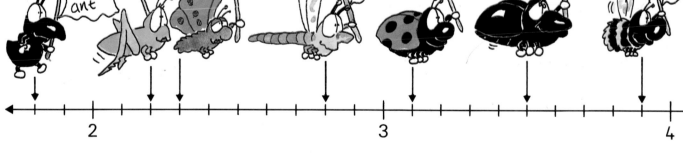

C

1. Copy and complete:

The ant is at 1·8
The grasshopper is at ____
The butterfly is at ____
The dragonfly is at ____
The ladybird is at ____
The beetle is at ____
The bee is at ____

2. Which insect is:

(a) 1·3 further on than the ant?
(b) 0·6 ahead of the grasshopper?
(c) 1·2 ahead of the butterfly?
(d) 0·7 further on than the dragonfly?
(e) 0·8 ahead of the ladybird?
(f) 0·4 ahead of the beetle?

A

You will need a decimal counting board and some counters to help you do these.

Remember to change 10 tenths for one unit if you need to.

1.	28·5 + 11·4	4.	18·6 + 53·8	7.	87·9 + 10·7	10.	46·7 + 13·6
2.	80·3 + 17·9	5.	18·4 + 74·2	8.	62·8 + 7·4	11.	42·3 + 29·9
3.	2·5 + 32·6	6.	49·4 + 8·1	9.	65·9 + 15·2	12.	56·8 + 19·8

B

Look at this sum: 12 + 3·6

We write 12 as 12·0 to keep the sum tidy.

```
  12·0
+  3·6
  15·6
```

12 + 3·6
Mmm – well
12 + 3 = 15.
So 12 + 3·6 = 15·6.

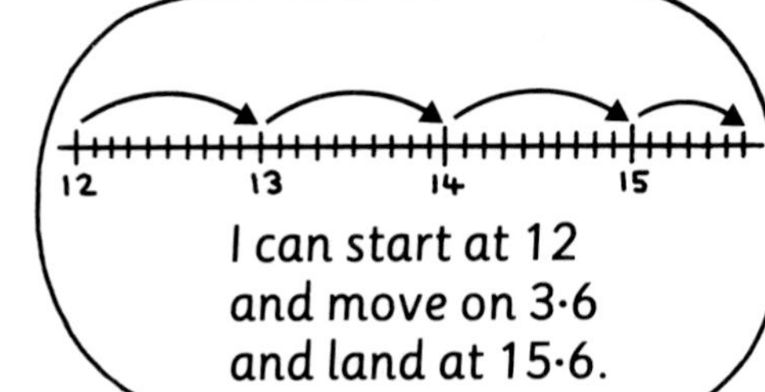

12
13
14
15
I can start at 12
and move on 3·6
and land at 15·6.

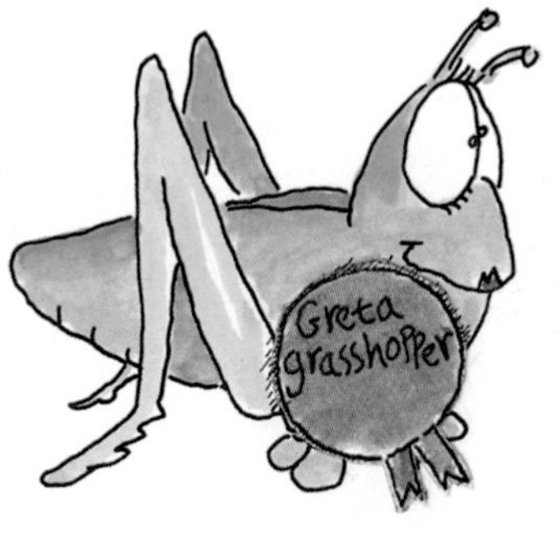

Adam, Greta and Billy each did the addition in a different way and all of them got it right. Bella Butterfly did not get the right answer. Can you see what she did wrong?

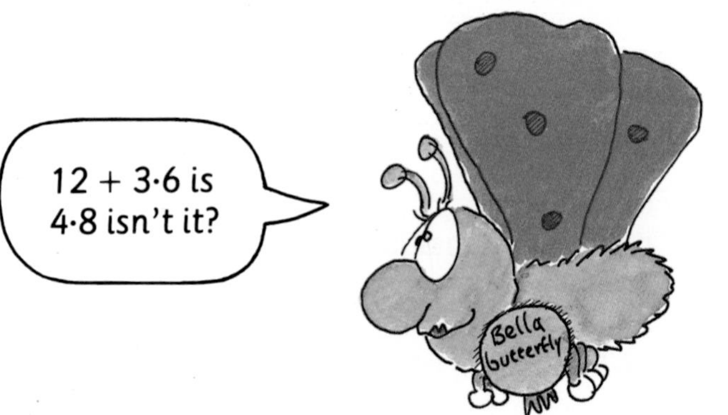

12 + 3·6 is
4·8 isn't it?
Bella
butterfly

Do these in your own way.

1. 4·2 + 3·7
2. 8·9 + 4
3. 6·2 + 12·3
4. 11 + 3·4
5. 21 + 3·8
6. 6·2 + 35
7. 12·5 + 0·6
8. 36 + 9·4
9. 20·4 + 2·5
10. 23 + 2·3

Bookworms

1. The county library has 8351 books on the shelves in the lending section of the adult library. 4696 books are out on loan. How many books are there altogether in this section?

2. How many books are in each of these sections of the library?

Reference section: 43 being repaired
2189 on the shelves

Children's section: 2014 out on loan
5198 on the shelves
75 being repaired

School section: 850 at Maple Leaf High
750 at County High
200 each at Moorhill, Beech Road and Gilby Park

3. Here are the figures for the number of books borrowed each month last year.

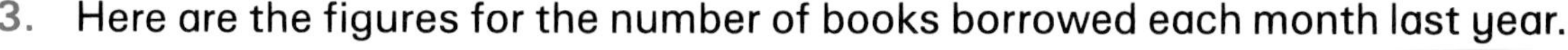

	Jan	Feb	March	April	May	June	July	Aug	Sept	Oct	Nov	Dec
Adults	3462	3874	4185	3980	3963	3844	3607	3886	4031	3964	3918	3218
Children	1941	2002	1861	1743	2162	1790	1863	2471	2194	1928	1654	1749

(a) How many books were borrowed altogether in January?
(b) How many more books were borrowed in September than May?
(c) How many books were borrowed altogether in October, November and December?

4. Some of the library books are in sets and are kept together on the same shelf.

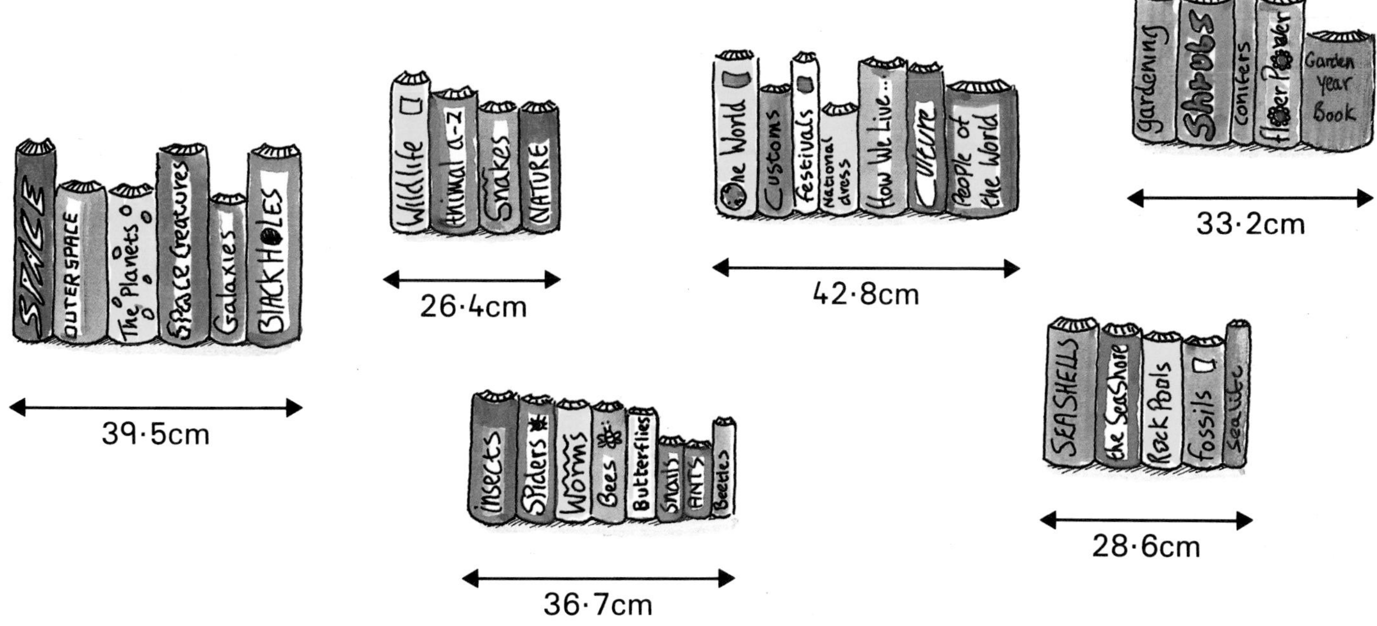

Work out and write down how these 6 sets of books can be put onto 3 shelves, each 70cm wide.

A

Here are some final scores.
For each game, work out who won and by how much.

Swimming
Don 479 Jim 321

Rowing
Louise 128 Leanne 536

Archery
Katy 5617 Aisha 2839

Cycling
Daryl 634 Joseph 270

Tiddlywinks
Ranee 5627 Suji 3408

Throwing
Ivan 4437 Darren 8219

Diving
Kerry 359 Susan 528

Skiing
Charles 8406 Terry 2131

B

Set these down carefully and then work them out.

Write down the answers in order of size with the letters shown (smallest first). What does it say?

B 3842 − 479
E 4362 − 9
E 9136 − 3000
K 5260 − 92
E 571 − 87
R 2004 − 108
O 1002 − 111

A 5832 − 900
R 429 − 37
R 4208 − 760
R 9063 − 87
C 1076 − 346
D 2131 − 7

C

1. To reach the final of the Tiddlywinks Flip, Bobby needs 6000 points. He has scored 4698 so far. How many more does he need?
2. The Scooter Trials take place on an 800m track.
   (a) George fell off his scooter 176m from the end. How far had he travelled?
   (b) When George fell off, Suzanne was 80m behind him. How far did Suzanne have to go to finish?
3. In the Horse Jumping Trials, all competitors start with 2000 points. Peter lost 210 time points, 180 jumping points and 20 style points. What is his score?
4. The Pole Vault record is 1 205cm. Samuel missed this record by 8cm. How high did he vault?

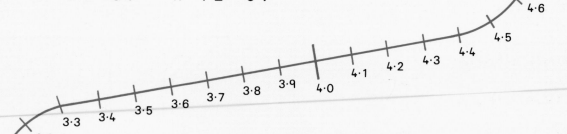

A

Do these subtractions.
Use the number line to help you.

1. 0·8 − 0·4
2. 0·7 − 0·2
3. 0·9 − 0·5
4. 0·8 − 0·6
5. 1·6 − 0·5
6. 1·4 − 0·7
7. 1·5 − 0·8
8. 1·8 − 0·9
9. 1·2 − 0·7

B

1. 4·6 − 1
2. 5·8 − 1
3. 4·8 − 1
4. 4·2 − 1
5. 5·4 − 2
6. 4·4 − 1·2
7. 5·3 − 1·1
8. 4·9 − 1·5
9. 5·4 − 1·6
10. 5·0 − 1·4

C

Now try these.

1. 1·7 − 0·5 = ____
2. 2·8 − 1·6 = ____
3. 5·5 − 2·2 = ____
4. 4·8 − 2·3 = ____
5. 5·9 − 3·5 = ____
6. 5·4 − 3·2 = ____
7. 5·6 − 4·6 = ____
8. 3·9 − 2·6 = ____
9. 4·8 − 4·1 = ____
10. 3·2 − 1·1 = ____

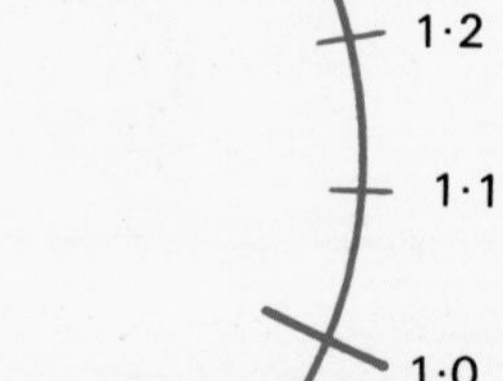

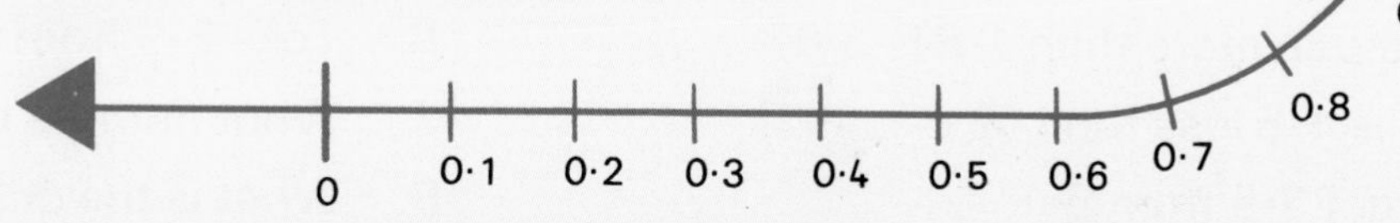

Decimal Exchange

A

Copy and complete these.

1. $\begin{array}{r} 3{\cdot}3 \\ -\ 1{\cdot}5 \\ \hline \\ \hline \end{array}$
2. $\begin{array}{r} 4{\cdot}2 \\ -\ 2{\cdot}6 \\ \hline \\ \hline \end{array}$
3. $\begin{array}{r} 4{\cdot}4 \\ -\ 3{\cdot}6 \\ \hline \\ \hline \end{array}$
4. $\begin{array}{r} 5{\cdot}4 \\ -\ 0{\cdot}9 \\ \hline \\ \hline \end{array}$
5. $\begin{array}{r} 3{\cdot}7 \\ -\ 1{\cdot}9 \\ \hline \\ \hline \end{array}$
6. $\begin{array}{r} 5{\cdot}0 \\ -\ 3{\cdot}5 \\ \hline \\ \hline \end{array}$
7. $\begin{array}{r} 4{\cdot}8 \\ -\ 2{\cdot}9 \\ \hline \\ \hline \end{array}$

B

Set these sums down like the ones above, and work out the answers.

1. 4·3 − 1·4
2. 5·2 − 2·5
3. 2·7 − 0·8
4. 7·0 − 5·5
5. 5·1 − 4·6
6. 4·6 − 2·9
7. 5·3 − 2·6
8. 6·0 − 3·1
9. 4·6 − 3·9
10. 5·5 − 3·7
11. 8·7 − 5·9
12. 7·3 − 5·6

C

1. Find the difference between 4·6 and 6·2.
2. How much more than 1·8 is 3·6?
3. What is 1·5 less than 4?
4. Subtract 3·5 from 6·1.
5. How much less than 7·5 is 3·9?
6. Take 5·9 from 9·5.
7. What number is 2·6 less than 5·2?
8. What is the difference between 1·4 and 4·1?

You will need the worksheet called Machine Records and a calculator.

A

1. Put the numbers 1 to 10 through this double machine. Use your worksheet to record your answers.

2. Now put the numbers 1 to 10 through this single machine. Use a calculator to help you.

3. What do you notice? Why do you think it happens?

B

1. Put the numbers 1 to 10 through this double machine. Use your worksheet to record your answers.

2. What single machine is the same as this machine? Check your answer with a calculator.

C

Look at this triple machine.

1. Copy and complete this table for it.

In			Out
1			
2			
3			
4			
5			
6			
7			
8			
9			
10			

2. Find as many single, double and triple machines as you can to do the same job.
3. Which machine do you find easiest to use?

Multiplying By A Hundred

You will need the worksheet called Machine Records and a calculator.

A

Do you remember the pattern for multiplying by 10?

Write down the answers to these.
Use your calculator to check the answers.

1. 10 × 57
2. 10 × 63
3. 10 × 49
4. 85 × 10
5. 10 × 36
6. 91 × 10
7. 10 × 75
8. 72 × 10

B

Look at this double machine.
Fill in a table for it.

In	Middle	Out
23		
45		
37		
64		
59		
78		

What single machine will do the same job? Check your answer with a calculator.

C

Now do these. Write the answers only.

1. 29 × 100
2. 36 × 100
3. 55 × 100
4. 62 × 100
5. 100 × 39
6. 100 × 47
7. 100 × 96
8. 100 × 88
9. 100 × 73
10. 100 × 64
11. 81 × 100
12. 40 × 100

D

Do you suppose the pattern works for multiplying even bigger numbers by 100?
Write down answers to these.

1. 391 × 100
2. 796 × 100
3. 100 × 805
4. 100 × 957
5. 100 × 489
6. 998 × 100

Check your predictions with a calculator.

You must not use a calculator for this page.

A

Draw a double machine which does the same job as each of these single machines.

Now use your double machines to work out these sums.

You could write: 57 $\xrightarrow{\times 2}$ 114 $\xrightarrow{\times 10}$ 1140

1. 57 × 20
2. 30 × 28
3. 31 × 40
4. 30 × 42
5. 20 × 98
6. 52 × 40
7. 30 × 39
8. 47 × 40

Change the order if you like.

B

Use double machines to work these out too.

1. 12 × 35
2. 18 × 27
3. 24 × 32
4. 15 × 43
5. 47 × 16
6. 38 × 14
7. 12 × 72
8. 18 × 59
9. 24 × 48

Three Ways

A

These children each chose a different way of doing their divisions. Look:

Hazel's way

96 ÷ 4

First we share the tens

```
    2
4 | 9 ¹6
```

Now we share the 16 units

```
    2  4
4 | 9 ¹6
```

Sam's way

96 ÷ 4

```
 9 6
 8 0  ← 20 groups of 4
 ---
 1 6
 1 6  ← 4 groups of 4
 ---
   0
```

The answer is 24 groups of 4

John's way

96 ÷ 4

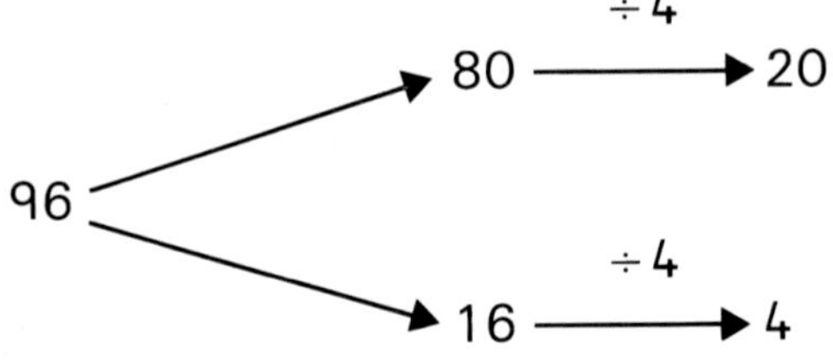

So 96 ÷ 4 is 24

Use Hazel's way for these.

1. 66 ÷ 2
2. 71 ÷ 3
3. 55 ÷ 5
4. 84 ÷ 4
5. 82 ÷ 3
6. 79 ÷ 4

Use Sam's way for these.

7. 78 ÷ 2
8. 97 ÷ 3
9. 77 ÷ 4
10. 82 ÷ 5
11. 59 ÷ 3
12. 61 ÷ 4

Use John's way for these.

13. 48 ÷ 2
14. 69 ÷ 3
15. 82 ÷ 4
16. 59 ÷ 5
17. 73 ÷ 3
18. 98 ÷ 4

B

Now choose any of the three ways to do these.

1. 53 ÷ 2
2. 79 ÷ 3
3. 81 ÷ 4
4. 90 ÷ 5
5. 62 ÷ 2
6. 58 ÷ 3
7. 49 ÷ 4
8. 93 ÷ 3
9. 89 ÷ 5
10. 77 ÷ 3
11. 67 ÷ 4
12. 56 ÷ 2

A

1. Rounders bases are sold in sets of 4. There are 81 rounders bases.
   (a) How many sets can be made?
   (b) How many bases left over?
2. There are 51 football socks in the shop. They are all identical.
   (a) How many pairs can be made?
   (b) How many socks left over?
3. Party poppers come in packs of 6. I want 75 poppers for the school disco.
   (a) How many packs must I buy?
   (b) How many extra poppers will I have?
4. Pencil crayons come in packs of 8. I want 90 pencil crayons.
   (a) How many packs must I buy?
   (b) How many extra crayons will I have?

B

1. 70 reflector strips shared between 7 bikes. How many strips on each bike?
2. For a game of 'Knock-down' you need 7 skittles and a ball. How many games can be played with 70 skittles?
3. Belto is a game for 5 players. How many games will be used if 75 children are playing at the same time?
4. The shopkeeper has 75 felt-tip pens and 5 plastic wallets. She puts an equal number of pens in each wallet. How many pens in each wallet?
5. A radio needs 4 batteries to make it play. If you have 70 batteries, how many radios can be made to play?
6. I have 70 photos to share between 4 albums. I want to put an equal number of photos in each one. How many photos will I have left over?
7. 55 tennis balls are packed in threes. How many packs can be made?
8. 55 books are to be put on 3 shelves. There are the same number of books on each shelf. How many books on each shelf?

A

Work out these divisions by sharing.
Write down your estimate before you work out your answer.

1. 642 ÷ 2 Estimate 300
2. 963 ÷ 3
3. 488 ÷ 4
4. 505 ÷ 5
5. 721 ÷ 3
6. 763 ÷ 4
7. 145 ÷ 5
8. 706 ÷ 3
9. 540 ÷ 4
10. 821 ÷ 5
11. 349 ÷ 3
12. 926 ÷ 4
13. 656 ÷ 5
14. 710 ÷ 2
15. 445 ÷ 5

B

Solve these sharing division problems.
Write down your estimate as you did before.

1. 350 small bags of compost are stored equally in 5 piles. How many bags are in each pile?
2. 450 rockery plants are planted equally into 3 display areas. How many in each area?
3. 964 plant pots are stored equally in 4 big boxes. How many are there in each box?

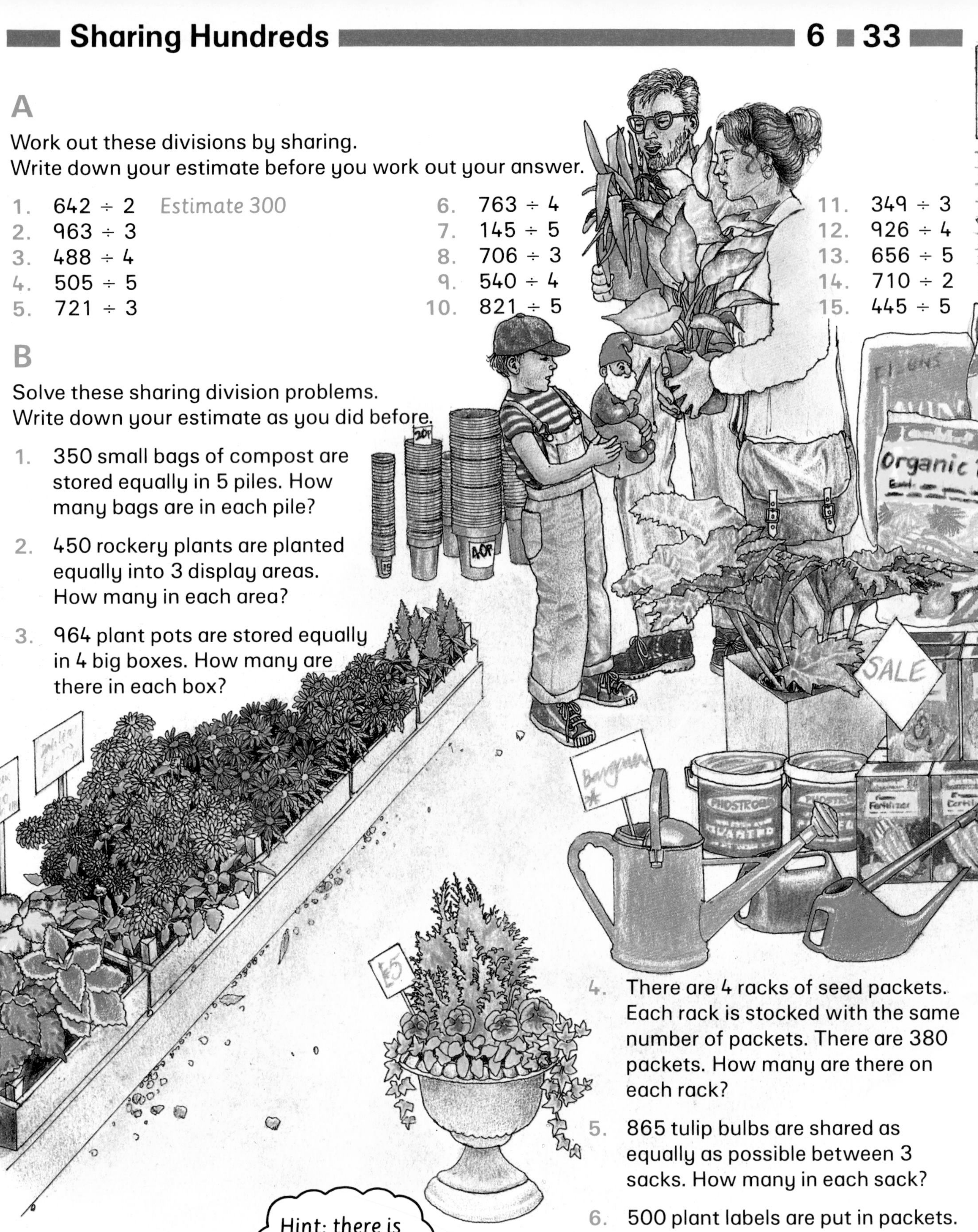

4. There are 4 racks of seed packets. Each rack is stocked with the same number of packets. There are 380 packets. How many are there on each rack?
5. 865 tulip bulbs are shared as equally as possible between 3 sacks. How many in each sack?
6. 500 plant labels are put in packets. There are an equal number in each packet. How many could there be in each packet?

Hint: there is more than one answer.

A

Work out these divisions by grouping. The first one is done for you.
Write down your estimate before you work out your answer.

1. 374 ÷ 3 Estimate 100

```
374
300 ——→ take away 100 groups of 3
 74
 60 ——→ take away 20 groups of 3
 14
 12 ——→ take away 4 groups of 3
r 2
```

We have taken away 124 groups of 3.
So 374 ÷ 3 = 124 r 2

2. 406 ÷ 4
3. 523 ÷ 5
4. 392 ÷ 3
5. 921 ÷ 3
6. 854 ÷ 4
7. 671 ÷ 5
8. 672 ÷ 3
9. 702 ÷ 3
10. 912 ÷ 4
11. 631 ÷ 3
12. 819 ÷ 4
13. 749 ÷ 3
14. 925 ÷ 5
15. 881 ÷ 4

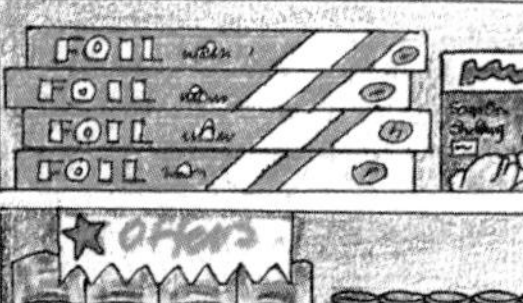

B

Solve these grouping division problems.
Write down your estimates as you did before.

1. Mrs Tate the shopkeeper ordered 480 razor blades. They come in packs of 5. How many packs did she get?
2. A salesman offered Mrs Tate a special deal of a pack of two bottles of shampoo for the price of one. She ordered 350 bottles. How many special offer packs did she get?
3. Hair slides are sold 4 on a card. Mrs Tate ordered 245 slides. How many cards did she get?
4. She ordered 212 fruit drinks in packs of 4. How many packs did she get?
5. Birthday cards come in packs of 5. Mrs Tate ordered 180 cards. How many packs did she get?
6. A customer ordered 130 chicken legs for a party. They come in packs of 4. How many packs did Mrs Tate order?

Estimation And Problems 6 ■ 33

 You will need a calculator.

Only work out the sum exactly if you need to.

A

Guess which number goes in each box.
Copy and complete these. Write 2, 3, 4 or 5 in the box.

1. 150 ÷ □ = 50
2. 200 ÷ □ = 50
3. 100 ÷ □ = 25
4. 150 ÷ □ = 30
5. 228 ÷ □ = 114
6. 184 ÷ □ = 46
7. 805 ÷ □ = 161
8. 408 ÷ □ = 136
9. 504 ÷ □ = 126
10. 594 ÷ □ = 198
11. 423 ÷ □ = 211 r 1
12. 757 ÷ □ = 151 r 2
13. 659 ÷ □ = 164 r 3
14. 827 ÷ □ = 275 r 2
15. 535 ÷ □ = 267 r 1

Now check your estimates with a calculator.

B

Use your calculator to help you solve these problems.
Remember to estimate first.

1. Cotton bobbins come in packs of 6. There are 750 bobbins for sale. How many packs are there?
2. Kim needs 100 buttons for her fancy dress costume. Buttons are sold on cards of 8. How many cards must she buy?
3. The stall holder sells 6 pairs of knitting needles together as a special offer. If she sells 192 pairs, how many special offers has she sold?
4. 675 patterns are displayed on 9 racks. There are the same number of patterns on each rack. How many patterns are on each rack?
5. Balls of wool are displayed on 7 shelves. Each shelf holds the same number of balls. There are 392 balls altogether. How many are there on each shelf?
6. Shaun needs 110 toggles. They are sold in packs of 8. How many packs must he buy?

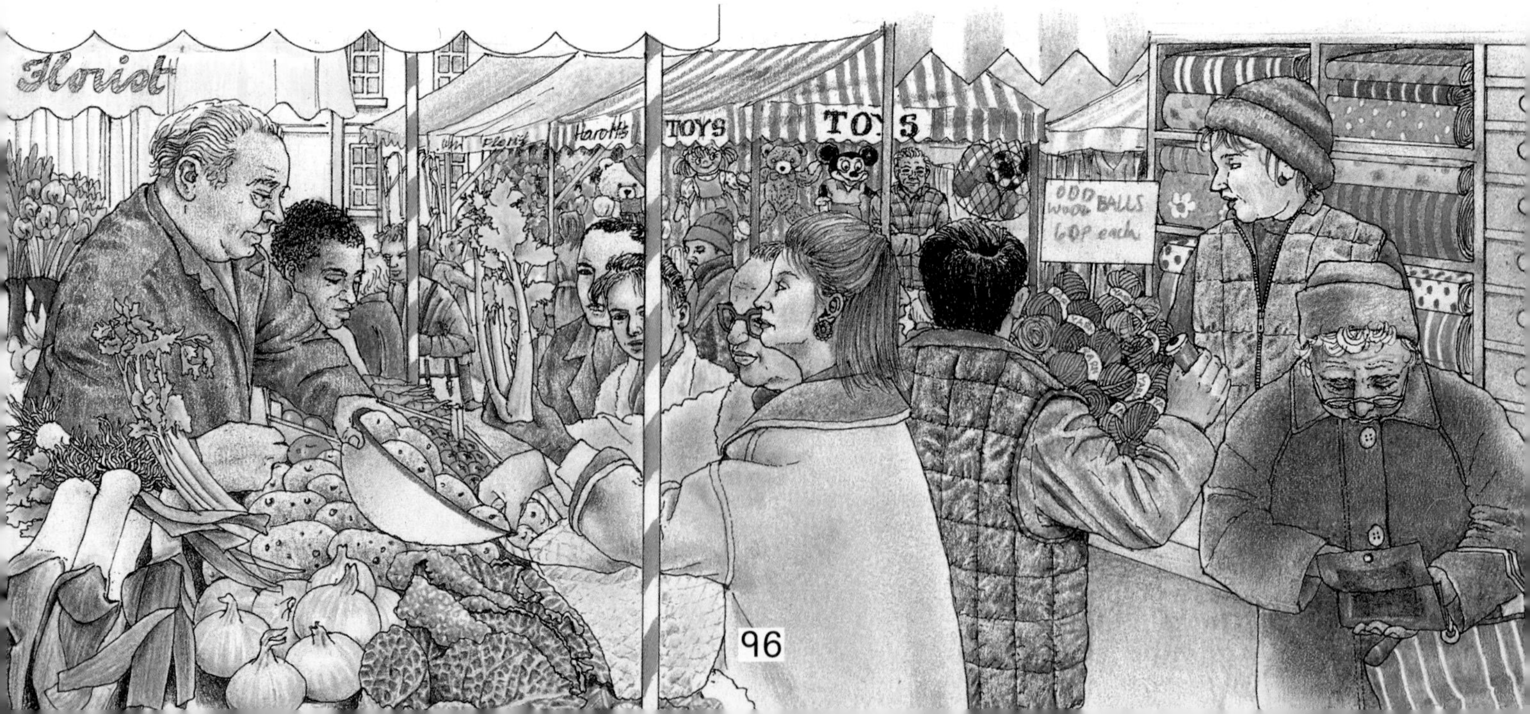

A

Put brackets in these sums to get two different answers.
Work out both answers for each sum and write them down.
Do not use a calculator.

1. $5 + 2 \times 3$
2. $6 + 4 \times 2$
3. $15 - 5 \times 2$
4. $20 - 5 \times 3$
5. $25 + 7 \times 2$
6. $25 - 7 \times 2$

Now guess which answer your calculator will get for each one.
Put a ring round the answer you choose.
Then check by doing it.

B

Write down what your calculator will get for these.

1. $7 + 3 \times 2$
2. $9 + 2 \times 5$
3. $1 + 7 \times 8$
4. $12 - 2 \times 2$
5. $10 - 3 \times 2$
6. $14 - 4 \times 3$

C

Use your calculator to work these out.

1. $42 + (19 \times 7)$
2. $(42 + 19) \times 7$
3. $(512 + 13) \times 9$
4. $512 + (13 \times 9)$
5. $512 - (13 \times 9)$
6. $(512 - 13) \times 9$
7. $873 - (24 \times 11)$
8. $(873 - 24) \times 11$
9. Which questions did you find easiest to do on your calculator?

D

Here are some harder ones to work out on your calculator.
The first one is started for you.

1. $(3 \times 7) + (8 \times 4)$
   $= \;21 \;+\; 32$
   $= \square$
2. $5 + (2 \times 6) + 8$
3. $9 \times (4 + 3) + 5$
4. $(8 + 5) - (2 + 6)$
5. $6 \times (3 + 8) \times 9$
6. $(8 + 3) \times (9 + 5)$
7. $(11 - 5) \times (12 - 7)$
8. $9 \times (15 - 8) \times 8$
9. $(12 + 6) \div (9 - 7)$

Can You Check It?

A

Work these out on your calculator.
Then do a check sum for each one.
Put right any mistakes you find!

1. 42 + 37 + 63
2. 49 + 35 + 23
3. 87 + 42 + 29
4. 61 + 92 + 85
5. 759 + 127
6. 199 + 806
7. 519 + 273
8. 312 + 386
9. 403 + 376 + 194
10. 312 + 569 + 196
11. 376 + 304 + 182 + 241
12. 406 + 203 + 297 + 494

B

Jimmy sometimes pushes the wrong buttons on his calculator.
Write down the check sum to see which of these must be wrong.

1. 327 + 866 = 1193
2. 733 + 581 = 1614
3. 302 + 235 + 772 = 1099
4. 386 + 862 + 621 = 1689
5. 378 + 103 + 606 = 1087
6. 541 + 742 + 997 = 1680
7. 423 + 249 + 266 + 366 = 1594
8. 297 + 133 + 582 + 123 = 1135
9. Which ones did Jimmy get right?

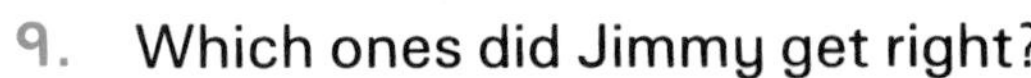

C

Look at this sum: 27 + 39 = 66.
The check sum is 30 + 40 = 70.
The check sum is out by 4.

Work these out on your calculator.
Then do a check sum for each one.
How far out is each check sum?

1. 33 + 22
2. 47 + 58
3. 32 + 67
4. 29 + 84
5. 53 + 68
6. 81 + 97
7. 66 + 77
8. 65 + 89
9. Which check sum is the nearest?
   Can you find a sum for which the check sum is exactly right?
10. Which check sum is the furthest out?
    Can you find one which is even further out?

Check It Again!

A

The check sum for 792 − 278 is 800 − 300 = 500. The exact answer is 514.

Work out the check sum for each of these.
Then find the exact answer using a calculator.

1. 69 − 18
2. 87 − 31
3. 71 − 46
4. 417 − 191
5. 686 − 324
6. 901 − 180

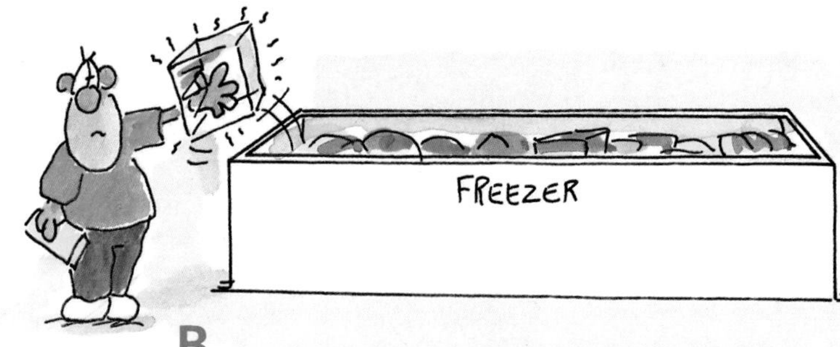

B

Which of these answers must be wrong?
Use only check sums to find out.

1. 808 − 191 = 415
2. 472 − 253 = 219
3. 792 − 233 = 559
4. 570 − 81 = 288
5. 903 − 161 = 742
6. 877 − 163 = 424
7. Which answers are correct? Use a calculator to find out.

C

The check sum for 6 × 471 is 6 × 500 = 3000. The exact answer is 2826.

Work out the check sum for each of these.
Then find the exact answer using a calculator.

1. 9 × 89
2. 8 × 16
3. 7 × 67
4. 6 × 482
5. 7 × 703
6. 8 × 542

D

Which of these answers must be wrong?
Use only check sums to find out.

1. 6 × 236 = 2496
2. 9 × 352 = 3168
3. 8 × 619 = 9102
4. 7 × 481 = 2167
5. 8 × 291 = 3028
6. 7 × 823 = 4801
7. Which answers are correct? Use a calculator to find out.

E

Look at your answers to Part C questions 1 to 3.

1. How far out was the check sum for each one?
2. Which one was nearest? Which one was furthest?
3. Can you find a multiplication for which the check sum is even further out?
4. Can you find a multiplication for which the check sum is exact?

A

You will need the worksheet called Machine Records.

1. Fill in this table on your worksheet for each of these machines. Copy the numbers carefully. Use your calculator.

In	Middle	Out
171		
228		
304		
361		
209		
285		

You need only write down the first two numbers after the decimal point if the answer is not a whole number.

2. Machine W is a lazy machine. Why do we call it lazy? Are any of the other three machines lazy?

B

Use the first sum to write down the answer to the second sum.
Think of the lazy machine.
Do not use your calculator.

1. 4872 ÷ 3 = 1624
   1624 × 3 =
2. 1572 × 17 = 26724
   26724 ÷ 17 =
3. 8613 × 23 = 198099
   198099 ÷ 23 =
4. 486 × 29 = 14094
   14094 ÷ 29 =
5. 17422 ÷ 31 = 562
   562 × 31 =
6. 17088 ÷ 24 = 712
   712 × 24 =

A

You will need the worksheet called Flow Chart For Primes, some squared paper and a calculator.

1. Write the numbers 1 to 96 on your squared paper in rows of 6, like this:

1	2	3	4	5	6
7	8	9	10	11	12

2. Use this number chart to work out the primes again with the flow chart. Do you find the same prime numbers?
3. Which columns have prime numbers in them? Write down the next four numbers after 100 which might be prime. Use your calculator to find out if they are primes.

Forget the first row, it spoils the pattern.

B

1. Write out a list of the multiples of 9 up to 90, like this:

9
18
27
↓

2. Now work out the next ten multiples of 9 after 90. Write about the patterns you can see.
3. Ivor wrote a flow chart for finding multiples of 9. Here it is:

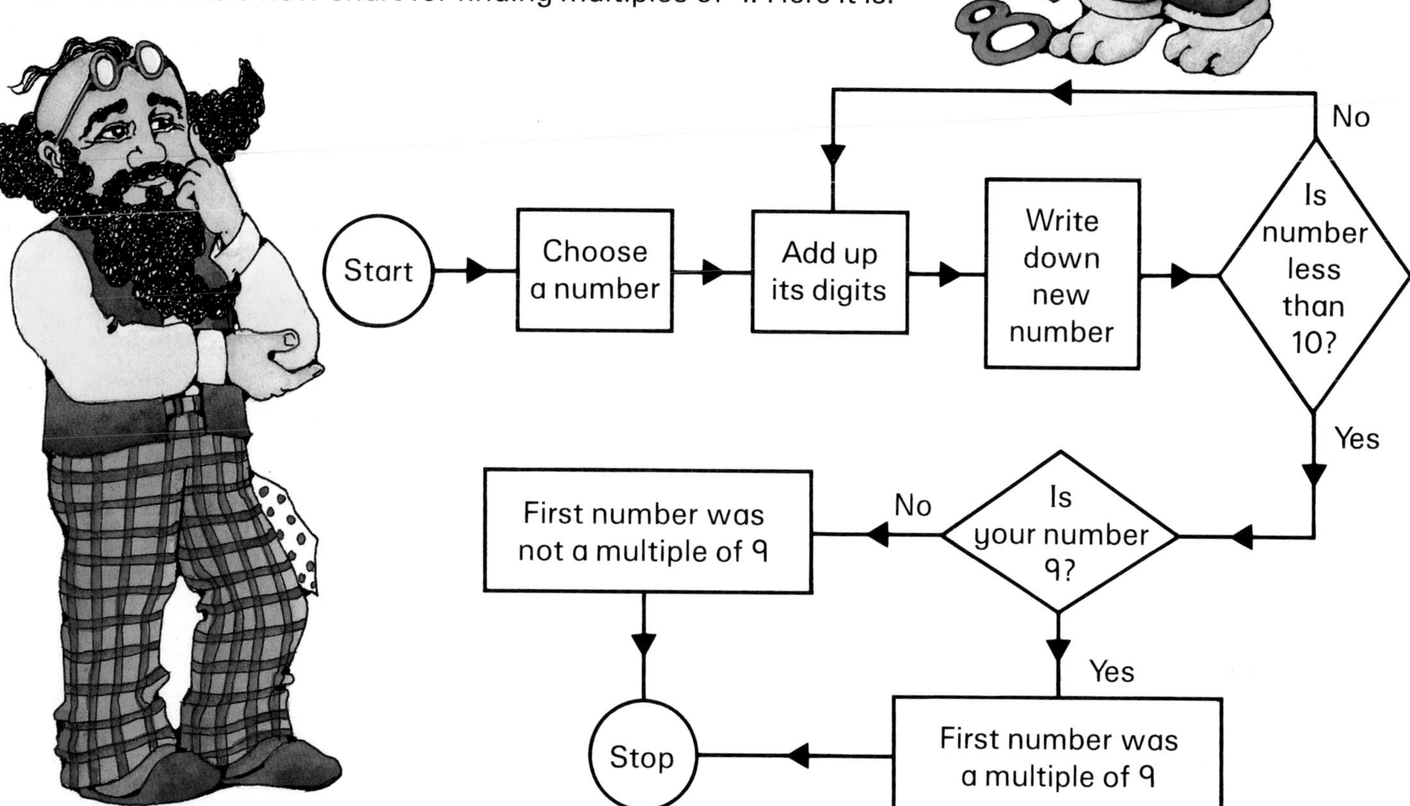

Choose 8 numbers between 100 and 1 000.
Use the flow chart to find out whether they are multiples of 9. Check with your calculator.

You will need a lot of Multilink cubes.
Work with your group.

1. Use the cubes to build the next caterpillar in this family of caterpillars.

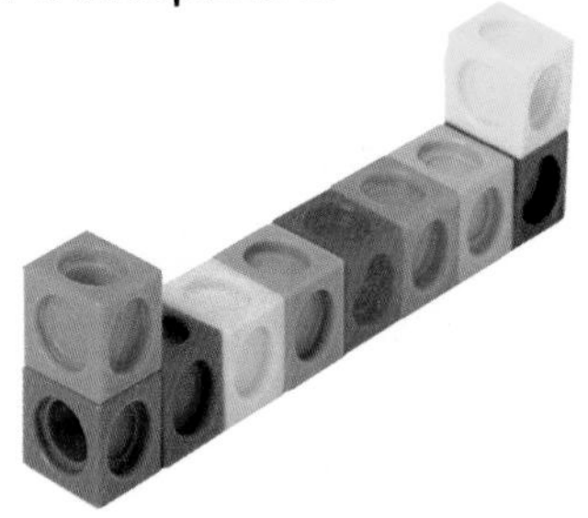

Then write the next seven numbers in this number pattern.

2. Do the same for each of these families.

Turtles:

Trees:

Houses:

Staircases:

3. Now build a family of three shapes of your own.
Draw a picture of each shape. Work out what the number pattern is.

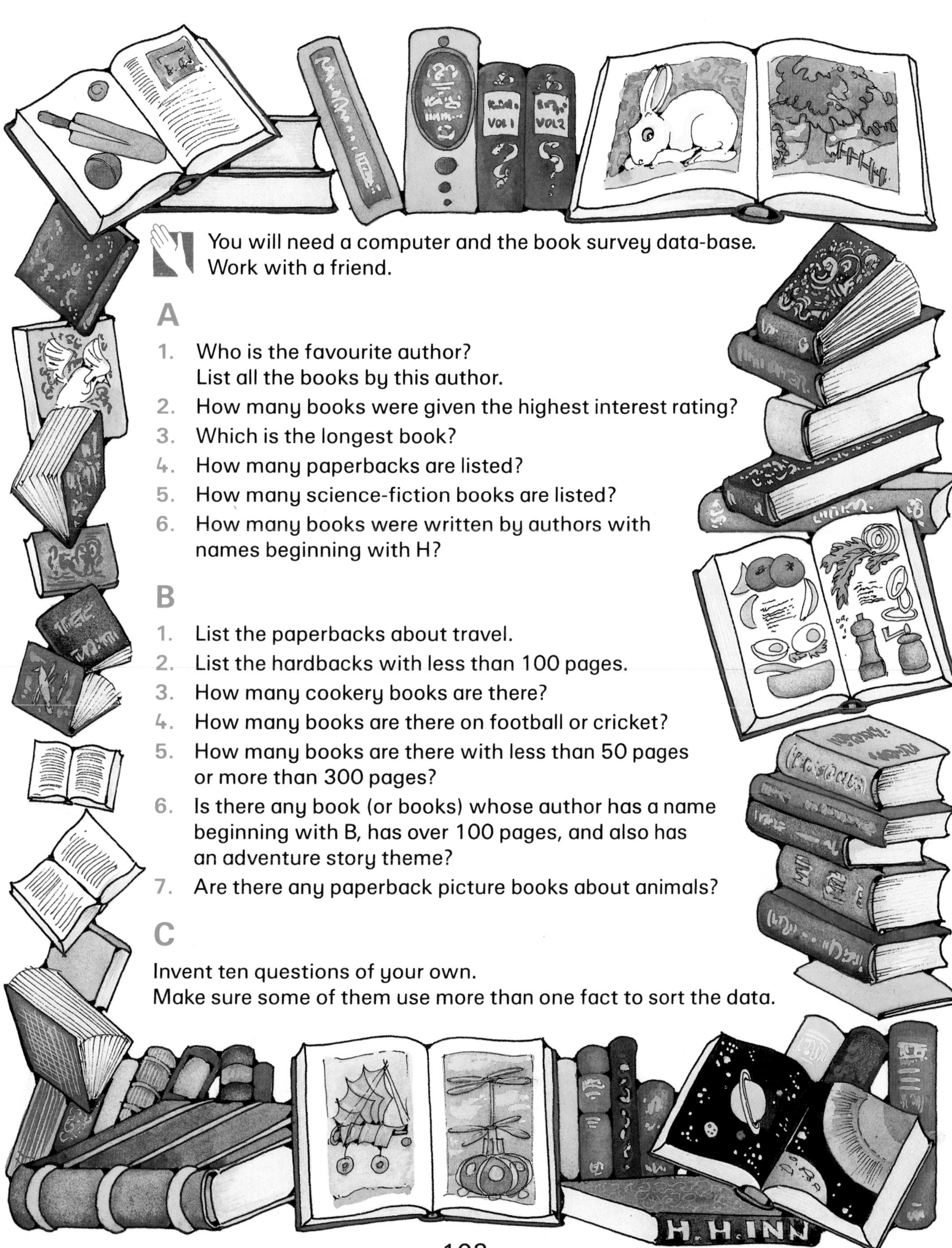

You will need a computer and the book survey data-base.
Work with a friend.

A

1. Who is the favourite author?
   List all the books by this author.
2. How many books were given the highest interest rating?
3. Which is the longest book?
4. How many paperbacks are listed?
5. How many science-fiction books are listed?
6. How many books were written by authors with names beginning with H?

B

1. List the paperbacks about travel.
2. List the hardbacks with less than 100 pages.
3. How many cookery books are there?
4. How many books are there on football or cricket?
5. How many books are there with less than 50 pages or more than 300 pages?
6. Is there any book (or books) whose author has a name beginning with B, has over 100 pages, and also has an adventure story theme?
7. Are there any paperback picture books about animals?

C

Invent ten questions of your own.
Make sure some of them use more than one fact to sort the data.

1. Mr Foley decided to paint all the woodwork on the outside of the house. He worked out that he would need 3 litres of undercoat at £6·30 per litre and 2 litres of gloss paint at £8·25 per litre. He also needed to buy a new paintbrush which cost £3·19.

   How much did it cost him altogether?

2. Mrs Foley wanted to decorate the hall. She had saved £80 to do it. She needed 10 rolls of wallpaper at £6·90 a roll, 2 litres of gloss paint at £8·25 per litre and 2 litres of emulsion paint at £4·80 a litre.

   (a) How much did this decorating cost?
   (b) Had she saved enough money?

3. Gemma wanted to make her bedroom look nice. Mum said she couldn't paint or wallpaper it as it was only done last year. Gemma persuaded Mum and Dad to buy a new duvet costing £12·99, a new duvet cover costing £19·95 and 2 new frilly pillowcases costing £8·25 each.

   Gemma then bought 4 metres of matching curtain material for herself at £4·90 per metre.

   (a) How much did Mum and Dad spend?
   (b) How much did Gemma spend?
   (c) How much did the bedroom cost altogether?

4. Grandma Foley wanted to put carpet tiles in her bathroom. The floor was 2 metres long and $1\frac{1}{2}$ metres wide. Carpet tiles were $\frac{1}{2}$m by $\frac{1}{2}$m and cost £3·70 each.

   How much did it cost Grandma to cover her bathroom floor?

You will need the worksheet called Shillings And Pence to help you do this page. You can also use counters and a counting board if you need to.

A

1.

	s	d
	1	11
+	1	6

2.

	s	d
	6	4
+	4	10

3.

	s	d
	15	5
+	4	5

4.

	s	d
	18	6
+	1	4

B

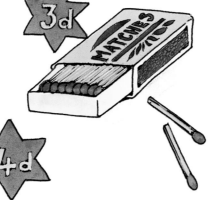

Find the cost of:

1. 5 boxes of matches.
2. 6 newspapers.
3. 3 magazines.
4. 10 postage stamps.

C

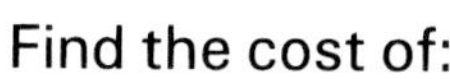

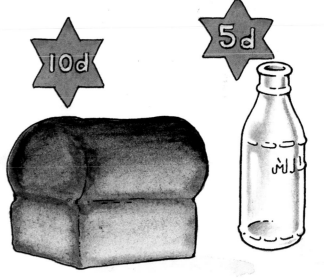

Find the cost of:

1. A packet of tea and a packet of sugar.
2. 2 loaves of bread and a bottle of milk.
3. One of each item in Part C.

D

1.

	£	s	d
	5	10	3
+	3	11	7

2.

	£	s	d
	2	19	4
+	12	13	6

3.

	£	s	d
	9	15	8
+	6	14	4

4.

	£	s	d
	5	19	9
+	2	13	1

Electrifying

You will need some squared paper.

Class 6 used a ready reckoner to work out the cost of cable at the DIY shop.
One metre of cable costs 60p.

1. Copy and complete this table:

Length of cable (m)	1	3	5
Cost in pence			

2. Get some squared paper and draw out this ready reckoner graph.
3. What does each step on the horizontal axis stand for?
4. What does each step on the vertical axis stand for?
5. Plot the results from your table onto your graph. Using a ruler, join all the crosses with a straight line to make a line graph. Be very careful.
6. Use your graph to find the cost of:
   (a) 4m of cable
   (b) 6m of cable
7. (a) Work out the cost of $1\frac{1}{2}$m of cable.
   (b) Plot this cost on your graph.
   (c) What do you notice?
8. Use your graph to find the cost of:
   (a) $3\frac{1}{2}$m of cable
   (b) $4\frac{1}{2}$m of cable
   (c) $5\frac{1}{2}$m of cable

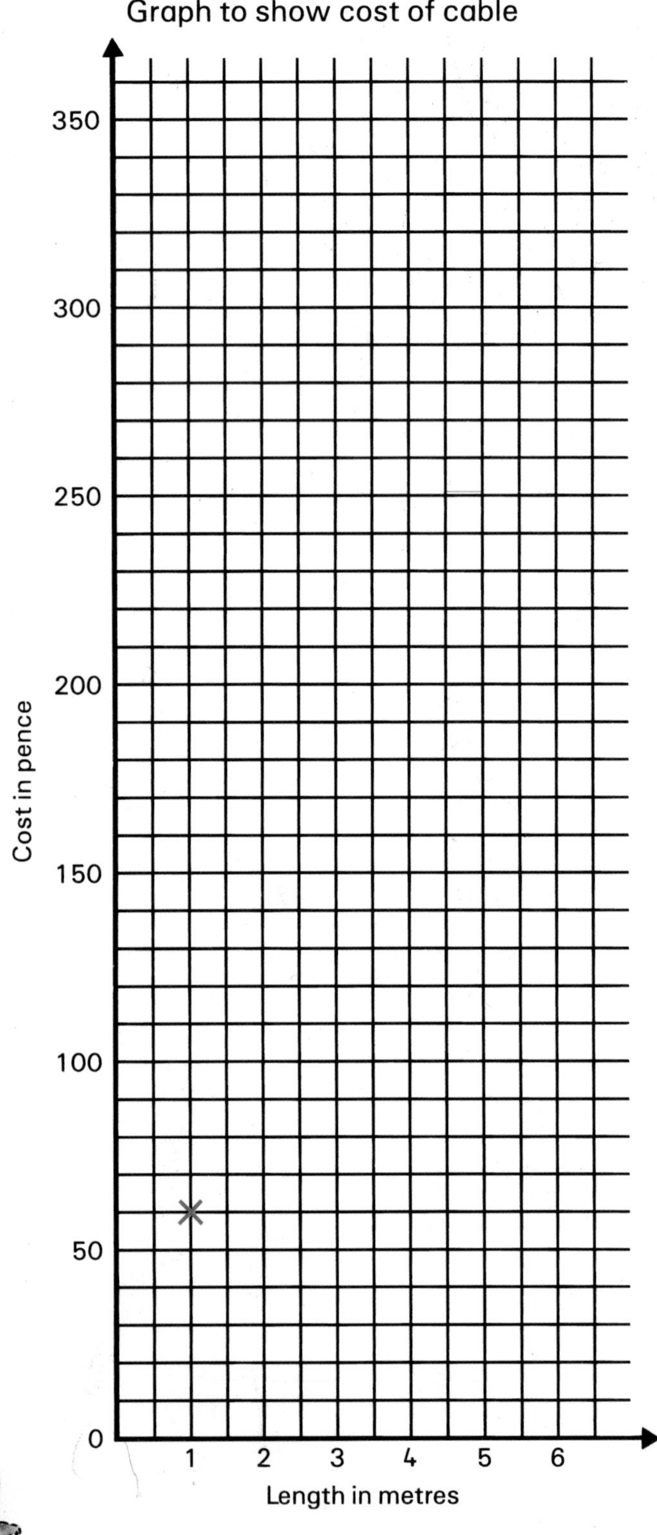

A

This page is about sorting events into these probabilities.

Probability 0	Probability 1	Probability $\frac{1}{2}$	Probability less than $\frac{1}{2}$	Probability more than $\frac{1}{2}$

Write the headings in your book.

Now write each of these under the right heading.

- You will have a daughter one day
- June 31st will be on a Friday in the year 2050
- You will marry one day
- You will leave school one day
- You throw an even number with a dice marked 1 to 6
- You will be seven next birthday
- You will go to bed tonight
- You will not watch any TV this week
- You will come to school tomorrow
- You draw a red card from a pack of cards
- You will go to a football match this weekend
- You will appear on TV one day
- You will learn to drive one day
- You will watch TV tonight
- You draw a ten from a pack of cards
- You will be a millionaire one day
- You throw an even number with a dice marked 1 to 10

B

Invent two more events for each of your headings.

You will need some coloured pencils and some squared paper.

A

Firtree School is going to design a new badge. The shape is decided.

It is

The tree can be red, green, blue, orange or brown.

The background can be white, yellow, or grey.

Draw a grid to show all the possibilities.
Start by drawing a 3 by 5 rectangle on squared paper.
Label it to show the possible colours. Then draw and colour each possible badge in its square on the grid.

B

You will need some squared paper, a dice marked 1, 2, 3, 4, 5, 6, and a dice marked 7, 8, 9, 10, 11, 12.

A game is played by throwing the dice, and adding together the two numbers on the dice to get the total score.
Make a grid, like the one you made before, to show the possible scores.

Answer these questions when you have finished.

1. What are the least likely scores?
2. What is the most likely score?
3. What numbers under 20 are impossible to score?
4. Invent some rules for a game using the grid and play it.

Bus number 56 goes from the Shopping Precinct to Callington.
Here is the timetable.

Shopping Precinct	06.00	06.30	then	09.00	then	19.00
Park Lane	06.04	06.34	every	09.04	every	19.04
Bus Station	06.11	06.41	half	09.11	hour	19.11
Fiveways	06.18	06.48	hour	09.18	until	19.18
Field Primary Sch.	06.25	06.55	until	09.25		19.25
Pool Road	06.35	07.05		09.35		19.35
Ridingsway	06.41	07.11		09.41		19.41
Callington	06.47	07.17		09.47		19.47

Look at the timetable carefully and answer the questions.

1. How long does the journey from the precinct to Callington take?

5. Ian has to be at Field Primary School by 9 o'clock. Which bus will he need to catch?

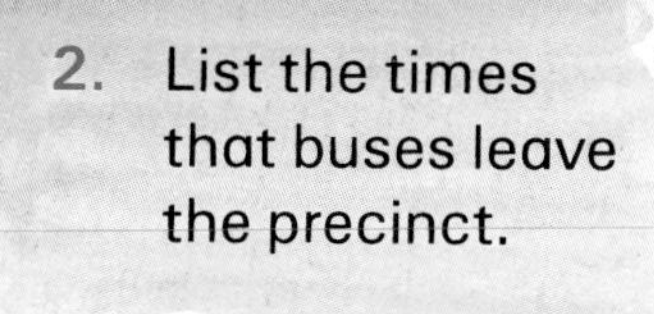

2. List the times that buses leave the precinct.

6. One day Ian missed the bus. He had to take the next one and was late for school. How late was he?

3. How many buses leave after midday?

7. Ian's mum works in Callington in the afternoons. She must be there by 1pm. Which bus should she catch?

4. When Ian leaves his home in Park Lane to visit his friend in Pool Road, he catches the 10.04 bus. What time does his bus reach Pool Road?

8. School finishes at 3.15pm. Which bus will Ian's friend be able to catch to take him home to Pool Road after school.

Travelling By Train

This timetable shows the times of the four trains which go from Puddleton to Tapton.

	First train	Second train	Third train	Fourth train
Puddleton	07.15	08.30	10.20	12.00
Overpool	07.40		10.45	12.25
Stepping Bridge (arr)	09.05	10.10	12.10	13.50
Stepping Bridge (dep)	09.15	10.25	12.20	14.00
Waterford	10.40		13.45	
Tapton	11.10	12.09	14.15	15.44

1. At what time does the first train leave Puddleton?
2. How long does the first train stay in Stepping Bridge?
3. Which train does not stop in Overpool?
4. How long does each train take to go from Puddleton to Tapton?
5. For how long is the second train on the move?
6. How many of the trains from Puddleton stop at Waterford?
7. If the fourth train did not leave Stepping Bridge until 14.15, when would it arrive in Tapton?
8. If you arrived at Stepping Bridge at noon, how long would you have to wait for the train for Tapton to leave?
9. Which train would you catch from Puddleton to be in Waterford just before 2 o'clock?
10. At what time would you catch a train from Overpool to be in Tapton before noon?

A Walk To The Park

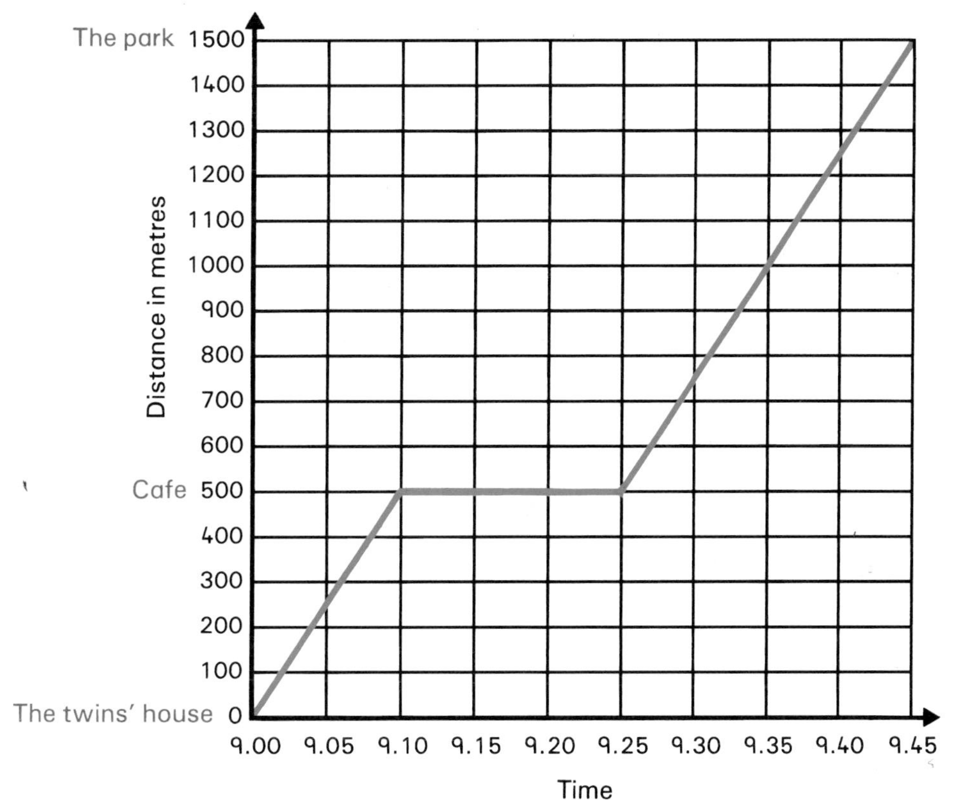

1. What does each step stand for on the time axis?
2. What does each step stand for on the distance axis?
3. How long did the twins take to reach the cafe?
4. How long did they stay there?
5. What time did they leave?
6. How far is it from the twins' house to the park?
7. How long did the twins take to walk from the cafe to the park?
8. How long did their whole journey take?
9. When the twins left the cafe, did they walk more quickly than before, slower than before, or at the same rate?

Kilograms And Grams

Work with a friend.

A

These weights are written as kilograms and grams.
Write them in grams.

1. 5kg 101g
2. 4kg 932g
3. 3kg 487g
4. 2kg 193g
5. 1kg 407g
6. 4kg 86g
7. 8kg 800g
8. 7kg 90g

These weights are written as grams.
Write them in kilograms and grams.

9. 4284g
10. 6194g
11. 1293g
12. 2751g
13. 1096g
14. 8216g
15. 4004g
16. 3949g

Remember,
1kg = 1000g.

B

You will need ten 100g weights
and four 50g weights.

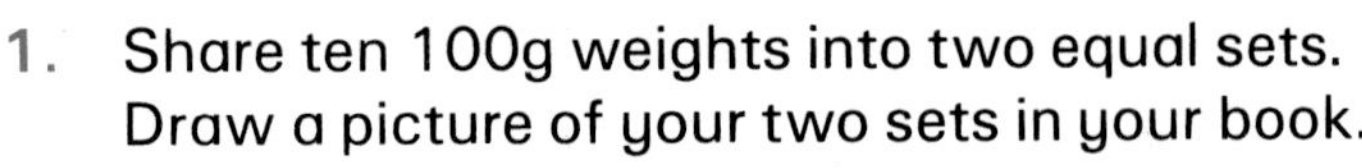

1. Share ten 100g weights into two equal sets.
Draw a picture of your two sets in your book.

2. Copy and complete.

I shared the weights into ________ sets.

Each set is ________ kg.

Each set weighs ________ g.

So $\frac{1}{2}$kg = $\frac{1}{2}$ of 1000g = 500g.

3. Now copy and complete the following.
Use your 50g weights to help you.

$\frac{1}{4}$kg = $\frac{1}{4}$ of 1000g = ________ g.

So $\frac{3}{4}$kg = $\frac{3}{4}$ of 1000g = ________ g.

Remember,
ten 100g make 1kg.

A

You will need ten 100g weights.

Remember, ten 100g weights equal a kilogram.

Share the weights into 5 equal sets. Copy and complete.

1. Each set is ______ of a kilogram.
2. $\frac{1}{5}$kg = $\frac{1}{5}$ of 1000g = ______ g
3. $\frac{2}{5}$kg = $\frac{2}{5}$ of 1000g = ______ g
4. $\frac{3}{5}$kg = $\frac{3}{5}$ of 1000g = ______ g
5. $\frac{4}{5}$kg = $\frac{4}{5}$ of 1000g = ______ g

Share the weights into 10 equal sets. Copy and complete.

6. Each set is ______ of a kilogram.
7. $\frac{1}{10}$kg = ______ g
8. $\frac{2}{10}$kg = ______ g
9. $\frac{3}{10}$kg = ______ g
10. $\frac{4}{10}$kg = ______ g
11. $\frac{5}{10}$kg = ______ g
12. $\frac{6}{10}$kg = ______ g
13. $\frac{7}{10}$kg = ______ g
14. $\frac{8}{10}$kg = ______ g
15. $\frac{9}{10}$kg = ______ g

Which of the answers in Part A are the same?

B

Copy and complete these tables.

1. A pack of chocolate weighs 200g, which is $\frac{1}{5}$kg.

Packs	Weight (g)	Weight (kg)
1	200g	$\frac{1}{5}$kg
2		
3		
4		
5		
6		$\frac{6}{5}$kg = $1\frac{1}{5}$kg
7		
8		

Remember, 5 packs weigh the same as 4 packs + 1 pack.

2. A pack of margarine weighs $\frac{1}{4}$kg.

Packs	Weight
1	$\frac{1}{4}$kg
2	_ kg
4	_ kg
8	_ kg
12	_ kg

3. Use your answers from question 2 to complete this table.

Packs	Weight
5	_ kg
6	_ kg
9	_ kg
10	_ kg
7	_ kg

A

Work out the total weights (a) in grams (b) in kilograms and grams of:

1. A tin of peas, a jar of coffee, a tin of soup, a packet of crisps and a packet of biscuits.
2. A bag of crisps, a tin of baked beans, a packet of cereal and a pot of jam.
3. A bar of chocolate, a packet of butter, a packet of biscuits, a packet of cheese and a tin of peas.

B

Copy and complete.

1. 1kg of flour costs ______ p
2. $\frac{1}{4}$kg of sugar costs ______ p
3. $\frac{1}{4}$kg of rice costs ______ p
4. $\frac{1}{2}$kg of teabags costs ______ p
5. 1kg of salt costs ______ p
6. 1kg of sweets costs ______ p

How much do each of these shopping lists cost?

7. 1kg of flour
$1\frac{1}{2}$kg of sugar
$\frac{1}{4}$kg of salt

8. 1kg of rice
$\frac{3}{4}$kg of sugar
$2\frac{1}{2}$kg of flour

9. $1\frac{1}{2}$kg of salt
2kg of sugar
$1\frac{1}{2}$kg of rice

10. 3kg of flour
$\frac{3}{4}$kg of sweets
$\frac{1}{2}$kg of teabags

Kitten Or Cat?

These ready reckoners are used by the warden of a cattery.
They show how much food is needed for different numbers of cats.

A

The dotted line shows that 3 kittens eat 600g of cat food.

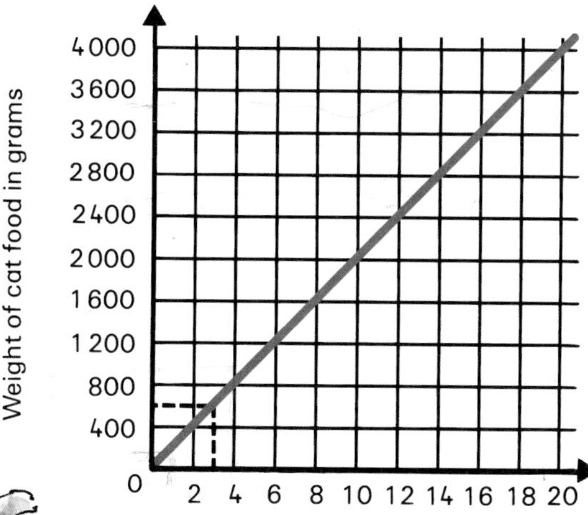

Copy and complete.

1. ☐ g feeds 4 kittens.
2. ☐ g feeds 16 kittens.
3. ☐ g feeds 1 kitten.
4. ☐ g feeds 19 kittens.
5. 1000g feeds ☐ kittens.
6. 2600g feeds ☐ kittens.
7. 3400g feeds ☐ kittens.

B

The adult cats eat much more.
This ready reckoner is in kilograms.
The dotted line shows that 6 adult cats eat $1\frac{1}{2}$kg of cat food.
Copy and complete.

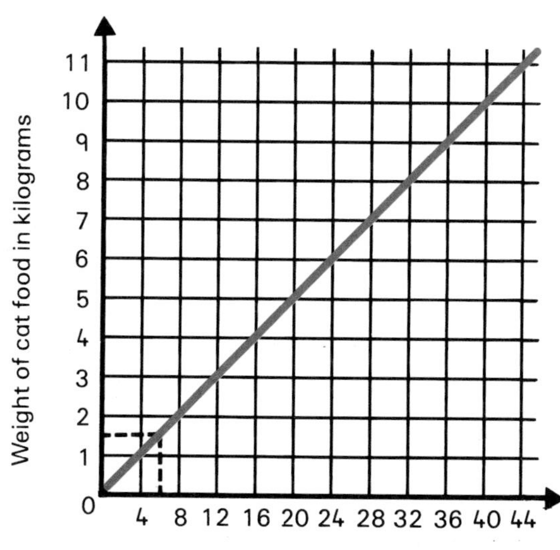

1. ☐ kg feeds 12 adult cats.
2. ☐ kg feeds 32 adult cats.
3. ☐ kg feeds 26 adult cats.
4. 4kg feeds ☐ adult cats.
5. 7kg feeds ☐ adult cats.
6. $2\frac{1}{2}$kg feeds ☐ adult cats.
7. $8\frac{1}{4}$kg feeds ☐ adult cats.

 You will need squared paper.

A

On a piece of squared paper draw two axes.
Number them from 0 to 15.

1. Mark the co-ordinate (2,12) like this:

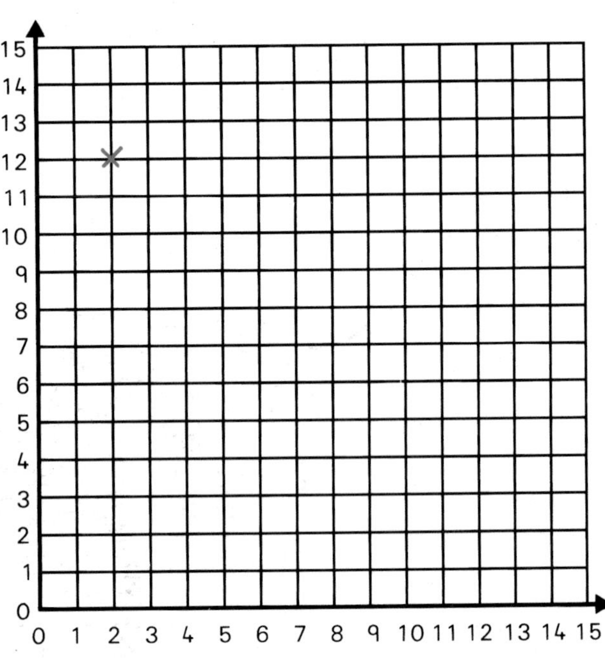

2. Mark (3,12) and join the points together.

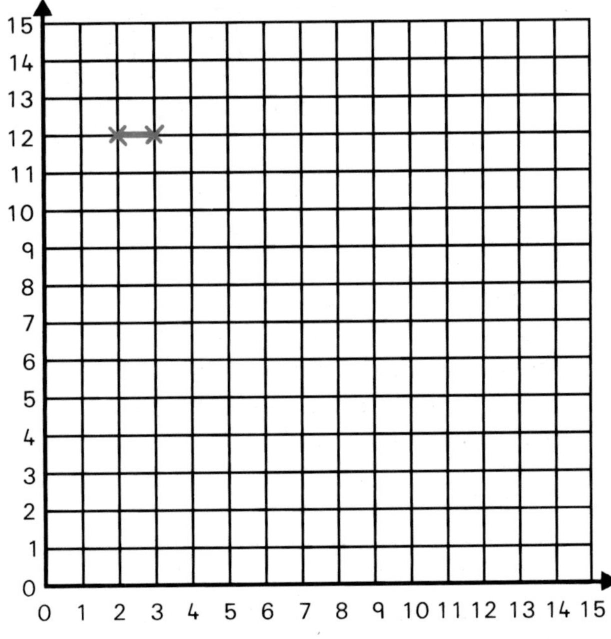

3. Mark (5,6) and join that to (3,12).

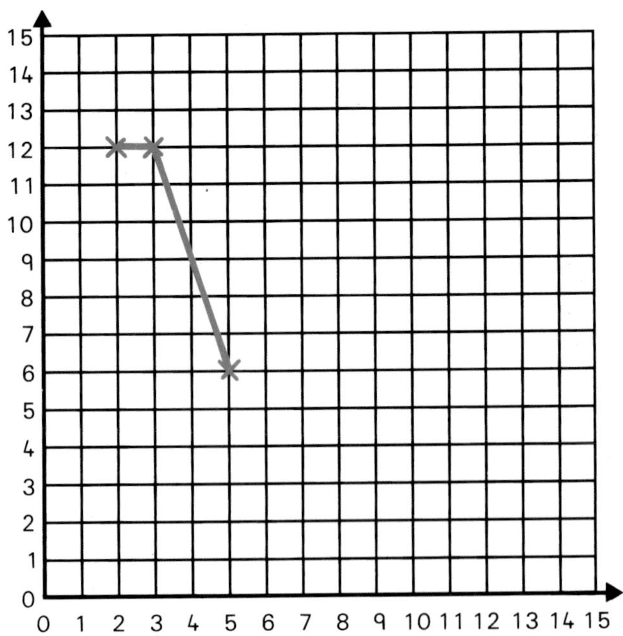

Now continue by adding these points.
Join them up as you go along.

4. (5,1)	9. (10,1)	14. (7,7)
5. (6,5)	10. (11,5)	15. (4,13)
6. (7,1)	11. (12,1)	16. (3,14)
7. (7,5)	12. (12,9)	17. (3,13)
8. (10,5)	13. (11,7)	18. (2,12)

19. What have you drawn?

B

On a piece of squared paper draw two axes.
Number them from 0 to 15.

1. Mark these points: (1,2), (4,2) and (1,5).
   Mark another point to make a square.
   Label the co-ordinates of this point.
   Draw the square.

Do the same for these squares:

2. (3,8), (3,12) and (7,12)
3. (10,11), (15,11) and (15,15)
4. (9,7), (11,5) and (11,7)
5. (7,0), (5,2) and (7,4)
6. (11,2), (13,1) and (12,4)

Careful, the last two are tricky!

More Co-ordinates

You will need squared paper.

A

Draw two axes on a piece of squared paper.
Number them from 0 to 15.
Copy this 'half tree' onto your grid.

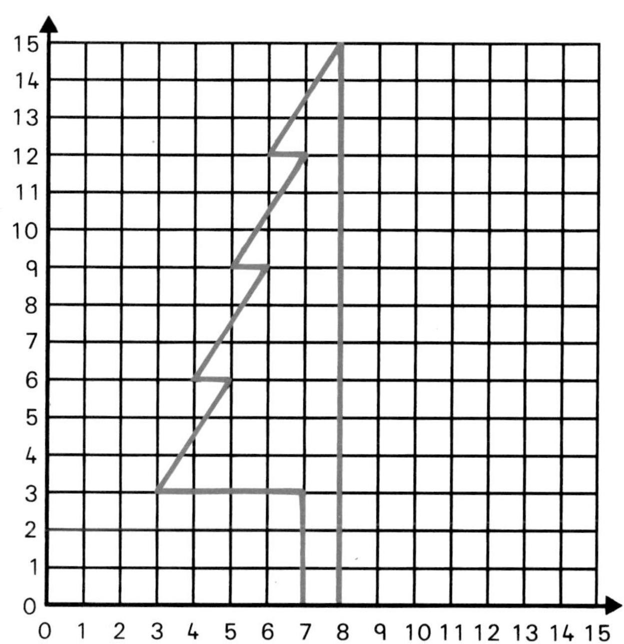

Write the co-ordinates of each point.
Draw the other half of the tree to match.
Write the co-ordinates of the points in that half also.

B

Draw two axes on a piece of squared paper.
Label both of them 0 to 15.

1. Draw this square:
   (3,2), (3,5), (6,2) and (6,5).
   Draw it again 2 squares to the right.
   (The squares should overlap.)
   Write down its new co-ordinates.
   What do you notice?
2. Draw this square:
   (1,6), (1,10), (5,6) and (5,10).
   Draw it again 5 squares up.
   Write down its new co-ordinates.
   What do you notice?
3. Draw this square:
   (12,5), (12,7), (14,5) and (14,7).
   Draw it again 5 squares down.
   Write down its new co-ordinates.
   What do you notice?
4. Draw this triangle:
   (12,10), (15,10) and (15,13).
   Draw it again 4 squares to the left.
   Write down its new co-ordinates.
   What do you notice?

Making Models

You will need some shapes to build with and some to draw round, paper, scissors and some sticky tape. You will also need the worksheet called Model Table.

Work with a friend.

A

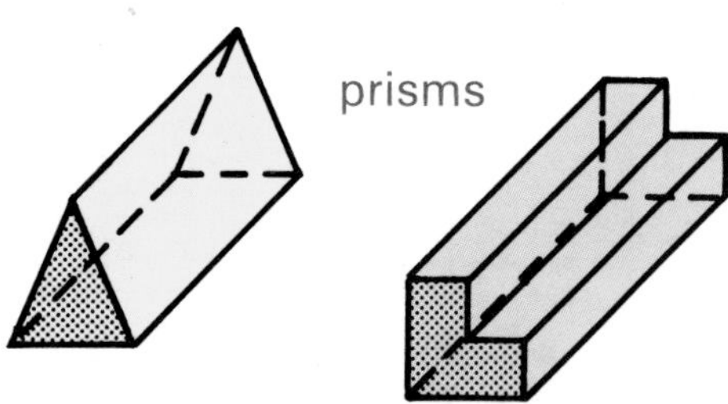

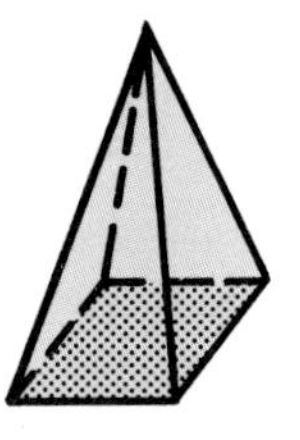

pyramids

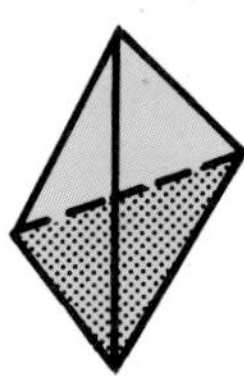

1. Use your shapes to build three different prisms.
   Sketch your models in your book.
   Write their names underneath.
2. Do the same again, but build three different pyramids.
3. Fill in the table on the worksheet for each of your shapes.

B

This is the net of a triangular pyramid.

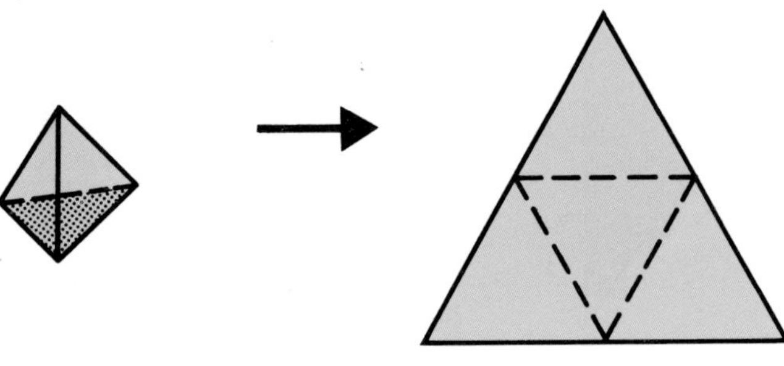

1. Make the nets of two other pyramids by drawing round shapes on your paper.
   Make a copy of each net in your book.
2. Cut out the nets. Build the solid shapes using sticky tape.
   Write the name of the shape in your book, next to the copy of its net.
3. Do the same for two prisms.

C

1. Write down the names of two different solid shapes that have 5 faces.
2. Write down the names of two different solid shapes that have 12 edges.
3. Write down the names of two different solid shapes that have 6 vertices.
4. What is another name for a square prism with all its edges the same length?